Choosing Forgiveness

CHOOSING FORGIVENESS

Unleash the Power
of God's Grace

FR. THOMAS BERG
and DR. TIMOTHY LOCK

Our Sunday Visitor
Huntington, Indiana

Nihil Obstat
Msgr. Michael Heintz, Ph.D.
Censor Librorum

Imprimatur
✠ Kevin C. Rhoades
Bishop of Fort Wayne-South Bend
October 6, 2021

The *Nihil Obstat* and *Imprimatur* are official declarations that a book is free from doctrinal or moral error. It is not implied that those who have granted the *Nihil Obstat* and *Imprimatur* agree with the contents, opinions, or statements expressed.

Our Sunday Visitor Publishing Division
Our Sunday Visitor, Inc.
200 Noll Plaza
Huntington, IN 46750
www.osv.com
1-800-348-2440

ISBN: 978-1-68192-653-7 (Inventory No. T2512)
1. RELIGION—Christian Living—Spiritual Growth.
2. SELF-HELP—Motivational & Inspirational.
3. RELIGION—Christianity—Catholic.
eISBN: 978-1-68192-654-4
LCCN: 2021952973

Cover design: Chelsea Alt
Cover art: Adobestock
Interior design: Amanda Falk

PRINTED IN THE UNITED STATES OF AMERICA

To our parents, who taught by example how to forgive

For Fr. Joseph Koterski, SJ
1953–2021
Teacher, Mentor, Priest, Friend
& Spiritual Father

Contents

Part Two
Forgiveness: The Process and the Possibilities

~

"Forgiveness is a strange thing. It can sometimes be easier to forgive our enemies than our friends. It can be hardest of all to forgive people we love."

— Fred Rogers

~

Introduction

So, Why Are You Reading This Book?

(Re)Discovering the Joy and Freedom of Forgiveness

You picked up this book for a reason.

Do you know what that reason is? You might know the reason very well: You're hurt and you're struggling to forgive someone, and you hope this book might help. Or perhaps the title jumped out at you, but you're not really sure why, *except* that you sense deep down that "Yeah ... forgiveness has always been tough for me. I wonder if I've ever actually forgiven _____ for _____."

Some hurts are your everyday, garden-variety irritations and agitations — the "slings and arrows" we endure for having to live in the company of other human beings who lose their tempers, get up on the wrong side of the bed, say nasty things, are ungrateful, selfish, and irritable.

Some hurts are of a magnitude that far transcend these — degradation, exploitation, abandonment, rejection, humiliation, racism, bullying, physical, sexual, or emotional abuse.

Whatever your reason for picking it up, we're confident this book can help.

To say that offering forgiveness is a challenge is an understatement. Forgiveness is tough! Forgiveness is often messy. Forgiveness doesn't feel good to most of us. And when it comes to the biggest, deepest hurts in life, forgiveness can seem impossible.

But we certainly can attest — and we hope you have experienced many times in your life — that with God's grace, even in those most difficult cases, forgiveness is possible. Consider for a moment the following true story, even if you're already familiar with it. It's one of the most humanly impossible cases of forgiveness you'll ever hear.

Immaculée's Story

Immaculée Ilibagiza was born in a small village in Rwanda, Africa, to a family belonging to the Tutsi ethnic group. She and her three brothers had a peaceful childhood, nurtured by their loving Catholic parents. In the spring of 1994, however, Immaculée's life changed forever.

On April 6 of that year, the plane carrying the Rwandan president — a Hutu — was shot down over the capital city of Kigali. His assassination sparked one of the most horrific genocides humanity has ever known. For the next three months,

Hutus massacred Tutsis throughout the country. Not even Immaculée's small, rural community was spared from the house-by-house slaughtering of men, women, and children. Her parents, two brothers, and many relatives were among those who were butchered.

Immaculée escaped death when she and seven other women huddled for ninety-one days in a hidden three-by-four-foot bathroom while the genocide raged outside. In her book *Left to Tell*, she recounts the incredible story not only of survival, but of inner transformation and the triumph of love over hate, and forgiveness over rage.

In the months after her escape from the genocide, Immaculée understood deep down that any possibility of healing — for herself personally or for her country — entailed forgiveness. She knew this is what God was prompting her to do. She returned to the devastated village of her childhood, where she visited the shallow graves of her mother and a brother, buried hastily after their gruesome deaths. Immaculée describes her battle that evening with rage and hatred:

> I tossed and turned for hours. I knew the devil was tempting me — that he was leading me away from the light of God, from the freedom of His forgiveness. ... I rolled out of bed and got down on my knees. "Forgive my evil thoughts, God," I prayed. "Please ... as You always have, take this pain from me and cleanse my heart. Fill me with the power of your love and forgiveness. Those who did these horrible things are still Your children, so let me help them, and help me to forgive them. Oh God, help me to *love* them."[1]

And with that prayer, peace returned, and she was able to sleep that night. The fierce desire to burn down every remaining Hutu household in her village was gone. She was back on the track of seeking the freedom of forgiveness. Her empathy and pity for her perpetrators were winning the day by God's grace.

Months later, she knew there was still something she needed to do. She had to confront and forgive the man who had killed her mother and brother — and had sought her out to kill her as well. It didn't take long to find out who was responsible, and in what prison camp he was being held.

His name was Felicien, formerly a successful Hutu businessman, and as a girl Immaculée had played together with his children. The warden brought him to her, half dragging him. Felicien was in tatters, emaciated and bruised. Immaculée broke into sobs at the sight of him — a man, as she understood at that moment, who had become the victim of his victims.

Felicien had been kneeling on the ground before her, but the warden forced him to his feet and commanded him to look Immaculée in the eye. She describes what happened next: "Felicien was sobbing. I could feel his shame. He looked up at me for only a moment, but our eyes met. I reached out, touched his hands lightly, and quietly said what I'd come to say: 'I forgive you.'"

After Felicien had been dragged back to his prison cell, the warden — in a mixture of amazement and disgust — confronted Immaculée. What on earth had she done? He had dragged in the prisoner — a man who had not only murdered her mother and brother, but had also hunted her down — so that she might spit in his face. Immaculée's response? "Forgiveness is all I have to offer."[2]

So how did she get there — to a place where all she had left inside for the killers was *forgiveness*? It was only possible, as Immaculée attests in *Left to Tell*, through prayer — prayer and an almighty struggle with hatred. As she shares in vivid detail, in the midst of the terror, in that bathroom with seven other women, in the degradation, humiliations, and misery, there was a battle raging in her heart.

She recounts that she got to the point where she tried, but unsuccessfully, to pray for the murderers. A demonic voice arose in her head to accuse her of hypocrisy every time she stumbled at those words of the Our Father: "... as we forgive those who trespass against us." She recalls:

> It was no use — my prayers felt hollow. A war had started in my soul, and I could no longer pray to a God of love with a heart full of hatred.
>
> I tried again, praying to Him to forgive the killers, but deep down I couldn't believe that they deserved it at all. It tormented me. ... I felt like I was praying for the devil. *Please open my heart, Lord, and show me how to forgive. I'm not strong enough to squash my hatred. ... My hatred is so heavy that it could crush me. Touch my heart, Lord, and show me how to forgive.*[3]

God answered her prayer. It came in a moment, in a sudden flash of the infinite tenderness of God, drawing on her own deep tenderness and empathy. "You are all my children," came the message to her heart: Immaculée, the women hiding with her, every one of the killers, the baby abandoned in the roadway whose desperate cries the women had to endure until the child finally died ... every Tutsi, every Hutu — all his children.

Immaculée experienced freedom at last. She was able to pray for the killers because she understood, intimately, that on the inside, they too were children — frightened, forsaken, crazed children. "And I could forgive a child," she suddenly realized.

≈

Immaculée's story illustrates so many beautiful things about forgiveness:

- That with God, forgiveness is always possible.
- That forgiveness often comes only as the fruit of great toil, and intense prayer.
- That forgiveness is normally not a one-and-done kind of thing — but rather, a process.
- That even if we want to forgive, we sometimes are not ready.
- That in forgiving the perpetrator, victims recover their own agency and dignity.
- That when you forgive someone, *you are set free.*

Especially that last point: freedom. Isn't that really why you picked up this book? Jesus assures us that "if the Son makes you free, you will be free indeed" (Jn 8:36 RSV-CE). But what about forgiving someone relying on our own human strength alone? Yes, it's possible. History has known different forms of forgiveness: the canceling of debts, pity, clemency, amnesty, exoneration, political pardon, and so on. You can find plenty of amazing stories of amazing human beings who, in pursuit of high humanitarian ideals and moved by empathy for their wrongdoers, have come to a place of forgiveness.

But it also seems that those stories are rare examples today in this historical moment that is characterized by unprecedented and obscene levels of partisanship, intolerance, rancor, and rage.

Christian forgiveness, *graced* forgiveness, forgiveness *in Christ* — this is really what this book is about. And just as in the experience of the early Church, even so today, this kind of radical forgiveness is an outlier. It's just as startling when you come across it today as it was at the beginning. And we need it more than ever.

So, what can this book offer you? Or more precisely, what can God's grace do in you and for you through the pages that follow?

Underlying our unforgiveness are emotional wounds — some small and transitory, some deep and life-changing. Whether it's the garden variety daily irritations, disappointments, or inconsiderateness of others that we must forgive, or the deeper hurts, they all leave their impact. So much so that we might imagine our heart as looking something like the lunar surface: pummeled with craters. Scientists tell us that these lunar craters range from microscopic in size to the largest one, which is some 180 miles in diameter. So even if — thanks be to God — you don't find yourself dealing with deep hurts, this book can help you find healing for the smaller hurts.

Of course, a lot of readers are dealing with major hurts. Any eventual healing of these wounds requires us, first of all, to acknowledge them. As we will see in the pages ahead, part of our deep resistance to forgiveness resides in our unwillingness to deal with the wounds that gave rise to the unforgiveness in the first place. But the deeper the hurts, the more intense the longing for the freedom forgiveness can give us.

We believe that, as you find the healing power of forgiveness, you can obtain the freedom you're looking for. We'd like to share with you a pathway to receiving the gift of forgiveness; the forgiveness you need to extend to any number of people in your life, and the gift of living free from the burden of sadness, resentment, and even hatred.

Some of the people we have accompanied have had to address their emotional trauma before they could approach the possibility of forgiveness. Others have had to forgive before they could address the trauma. If you are not ready or not in need of addressing significant traumas, this book can still be applied to the ordinary emotional travails of everyday life.

As you journey through the chapters that follow, we invite

you in particular:

- To read the chapters in order — no matter how much you might be tempted to jump right to chapter 6 where we lead readers through a four-step process of forgiveness. We have deliberately structured the book as Part One and Part Two. Part One, in which we explore the very nature of forgiveness and how God can empower us to forgive, can be enormously helpful if you are to fully apply to your own life the process of forgiveness that we explore in Part Two.

- To make good use of the reflection questions that appear at the end of each chapter in Part One. These questions will get you ready to put into practice the steps to forgiveness that we feature in Part Two.

- To allow the Holy Spirit to speak to you through the stories of forgiveness that you will encounter throughout the book. We're convinced that forgiveness is above all a *grace* — a gift that Jesus wants to give us. Use this book to lean on him, to allow him to lead you on a path of forgiveness and healing of the hurts in your life. If you are dealing with a major area of hurt in your life, you might even want to set aside some time away. Take this book with you and use it almost as a guided retreat in which you open yourself to the healing and freedom our Lord can lead you to through these pages.

- To discover or rediscover the joy that comes from the freedom God can give us in forgiveness. As the adage says, "To forgive is to set a prisoner free, and to discover that the prisoner was you." Indeed. Perhaps you've tasted that freedom before, and now you want it again. Be confident that our Lord also wants to lead you to that place of interior freedom and joy.

- To come to a much deeper understanding of the profound spiritual significance of forgiveness — an act by which we are united to God, do something utterly God-like, and through which he makes us holy. You will see, too, that forgiveness can also become a supreme act of worship and glory for God.
- Finally, to read the Afterword and join us in a consideration of how the pursuit of forgiveness and reconciliation within the practices of restorative justice can bring about deeper healing within the context of the Church's crisis of sexual abuse.

Sound like a plan? If you're ready, then let's roll.

Part One

Forgiveness: The Challenge and the Grace

Chapter 1
Getting at the Root

What Does It Mean to Forgive?

You must bear with me.
Pray you now, forget and forgive.

— *Shakespeare*, King Lear, *Act 4, Scene 7*

Merriam-Webster defines "to forgive" as "to cease to feel resentment." That is, in fact, a very common internal reaction when we forgive. Yet, *ceasing to feel something* is very different from *making a choice* — an act of the will. And if forgiveness is anything, it is most certainly an act of the will. So what, exactly, is forgiveness? What is it that we are doing when we forgive? How best to describe that peculiar act of the will we call forgiveness?

Forgiveness: What It Is and What It Is Not

If you asked ten different people to define forgiveness, you'd likely get ten different answers. Why this confusion? Some notion of forgiveness seems to be present in many cultures, at least as far back as the Greco-Roman world, and in many world religions. It is present in some form within Judaism before it becomes a touchstone of Christianity. Within all these contexts, it can be and has been defined in different ways and with different nuances. It is at least related to the concepts of pardon, debt cancellation, mercy, limiting the retribution rights of an offended party, acknowledging that a penalty has been paid, and so on.

There has also been considerable debate among scholars as to whether interpersonal forgiveness as we know it today is not more of a modern development.[1] But all this is a conversation for another day and beyond the aims of our book. Allow us then, in this chapter, to contribute the fruit of our own reflection and pastoral experience and share with you our own understanding of what it means to forgive, both on a human level and aided by grace.

But before we explain, we have to clear up some misconceptions.

Forgiveness is not declaring that the offense did not happen. It's not letting someone off the hook or renouncing the possibility of justice. Nor is it the same as reconciliation (to be treated in a later chapter). Nor is forgiveness a matter of just "getting over" something. Forgiveness is not ignoring the hurt and declaring, "It doesn't matter."

Forgiveness is not pushing something away or pretending

it didn't happen. The popular proverb — possibly originating in Shakespeare's *King Lear*, but also present in Cervantes's *Don Quixote* — instructs us to "forgive and forget." Yet it's usually offered to the offended party as an invitation to act as if nothing happened or to pretend to forget the offense. But neither acting as if it never happened, nor pretending to forget, has anything to do with genuine forgiveness.

In fact, the invitation to forgive and forget isn't healthy when dealing with a situation that warrants forgiveness. Once the heat of the moment passes, eventually our strong emotions — even the strongest, like hate — will tend to simmer down. We suspect this relative recovery of our baseline state is often mistaken for forgiveness: "Yeah, I guess I got over it." But what's missing here is the very *positive intentional act* of the will that constitutes genuine forgiveness. To forgive is a choice — an act we elicit from our very core with our reason, will, and emotions in response to grace.[2]

Letting Go — but of What, Exactly?

Many people describe forgiving as a "letting go." That definitely points us in the right direction for uncovering the true nature of forgiveness. It seems forgiving entails a renunciation — but renunciation of what? Forgiveness, it would also seem, is frequently experienced as a surrendering of something we have ardently yearned for, but now forsake. Renunciation, forsaking, letting go — but of what? If we really check our gut on this, we can be pretty sure that it's *something about the person* who has offended us, *something we want* from that person.

Is it justice? But the desire for justice is, in principle, a well-ordered desire.[3] To want justice is a sound and healthy desire; it can even become an essential part of healing. In fact, it is quite possible to both forgive someone *and* want to see justice served, as in those cases when the perpetrator's offense to us has been criminal.

So forgiveness cannot mean the renunciation of the desire for justice.

What it seems we are looking for when another has inflicted an emotional wound upon us is a kind of restitution. Restitution is the restoration of something lost or stolen: materially, personally, interpersonally, or even spiritually.[4] We are all of equal worth and deserving of equal respect. When one person offends another, their relationship loses the harmony and equilibrium to which we are naturally inclined in social relations. Social equilibrium and harmonious engagement — even with strangers — is a key ingredient of human flourishing. If we think of human flourishing as the fulfilling of our potential — principally through reason and the pursuit of virtue — on a gradual path of becoming what God intended us to be, we can understand that harmonious and healthy relationships with others are a primary manifestation of a flourishing human life.

Human flourishing is fulfilling our potential principally through reason and the pursuit of virtue on a gradual path of becoming what God intended us to be.

So on a deep level, what we want from the offender is some word, gesture, or action (such as an apology), or at the very least some acknowledgment of the offense, that will go in the direction of restoring that equilibrium between us.

In order to more deeply understand the answer to our question — What do we let go of in forgiving? — let's consider what we get in an *apology*. We might find insight there that will help reveal the essence of what forgiveness actually is.

Forgiveness and Personal Validation

A real, heartfelt apology, an authentic apology, is a balm to a wound. Apologies are personally and deeply empowering. They go deep, right to the heart. Their impact normally lands powerfully in the core of our self. What an apology packs for us is something every human being longs for by nature, something emerging from deep within our psyche: *personal validation* — the recognition that we are valuable, that our feelings and opinions matter.

In its simplest form, validation is both an emotional recognition and a cognitive (intellectual) recognition. Emotionally, validation communicates: I see you; I see your internal experience; I see the injustice that's occurred; I see the emotions that you feel, and I say that you, and what you have experienced, *matter*. Cognitively, validation communicates: I see your thought process; I see your logic, and I say that you are sound, you are reasonable, you are rational, you make sense.

Validation as such does not necessarily communicate belief in particular elements of the person's story, especially when this involves allegations against another. It does, however, communicate *acceptance* of the person and what they have, or at least believe they have, experienced. As human beings, we have a deep, deep need rooted profoundly in our human nature for such acceptance. That's why validation, particularly when delivered in the form of a sincere apology, can be so powerful.[5]

Validation says: You are worthy; you have dignity; you are deserving of my respect and veneration. Simply to look someone in the eye and listen attentively sends the message: I see you; I hear you; I am with you; you are worthy of being heard, loved, and respected. This is validation, and there are endless ways to validate another human being. Children, especially, thrive on it.

So an apology gives us validation on multiple levels. First, it offers validation of the reality of the offense: It says, essentially, "the offense did actually happen; it's not something you misinterpreted or made up." Second, an apology validates the fact that the offense has had a certain fallout. In one way, the validation refers to the situation, and in another way, it refers to the offended party's personal experience of the situation.

Personal validation — which includes the profound message of one's worth and the communication of one's worthiness of honor and respect — is hugely rewarding emotionally and psychologically.[6] Validation elicits a swell of good feelings. Validation reminds us of the depth of our worth. Validation provides an echo, as it were, of the fact that we are children of the heavenly Father who has loved us into existence with an infinite love. While the legitimate need for validation can easily grow into an imbalanced need for approval or dependency on another, the same could be said about the legitimate need for exercise that can easily grow into obsession about health and fitness. Nevertheless, both legitimate needs, in moderation, can be very good and even vital to our flourishing. In itself, validation of our worth and the emotional affirmation we derive from it are both necessary ingredients of human well-being throughout our lives.

Forgiveness and the Recovery of Interpersonal Equilibrium

As we have seen, an apology says quite simply: "You are right." It is a supreme form of validation. An apology also says: "I was wrong." In this exchange, the broken relationship is calibrated; the rush of personal validation displaces the personal, emotional, psychological invalidation caused by the hurt. A certain degree of equilibrium in this relationship, if not perhaps complete reconciliation, can now be recovered. The strong validation entailed in an apology, neutralizing the interpersonal tension, wonderfully restores that equilibrium or at least contributes significantly to it.

When someone offers an apology, and we feel this validation, we can easily accept the apology. We can reply: "I forgive you." However, when we have been hurt and the perpetrator is not offering an apology, we are left with this imbalance or instability in the relationship. We feel alone with the effects of the offense. Deep within, where we most mirror the image of the God who created us, we feel the violation of our dignity. The painful circumstances can give rise in us to unforgiveness. But from this place, forgiveness can also be born. Somewhere in this deep, dark place in our hearts, we have a choice: to hold on to the hurt, or to enter the unchartered territory of seeking release — not verbally, but internally.

Said another way, even lacking an apology from the perpetrator, we can achieve a similar recovery of equilibrium in forgiveness. This is because we can choose to forgive. In forgiving, *I am freely, supremely, and mightily renouncing the demand that the offender validate me by acknowledging the harm done to me.* I forgo that deep yearning for what would have been a very intense experience of validation. I take a leap of faith from the safety of holding on to anger, to the vulnerability of letting go. Note that this is more than a passive response. It's the active response of stepping out in forgiveness.

But here we must point out something of the greatest significance in the battle to forgive. In this supreme exercise of our freedom, we nonetheless experience another sort of validation, independent of the perpetrator's validation. We receive a deeply charged experience of self-worth: "Yes, *you* were wrong; *I* was right. And I freely renounce my need for your validation of my worth as a person." Because we are able to experience the deeper truth of our own dignity, we free the perpetrator from this obligation. This process can even potentially free us internally from our own craving for validation. In forgoing the need for the perpetrator's validation, we deeply experience our own true, God-given dignity and worth. And we regain control of a sense of equilibrium in our relationship with the perpetrator. In a word, trauma destabilizes and validation restabilizes.

It's worth noting here that we are not speaking of mere self-affirmation, a sometimes-problematic experience that can be the fruit of pride or an otherwise ill-conceived sense of self-importance or assertion of power. In referring here to the self-worth we can experience through validation, we are touching something that, under the guidance of grace, is more a grounding in our human dignity. For Christians, this self-affirmation can be a profound experience of their identity as a beloved daughter or son of the Father in Christ.

> *This intimate affirmation of my being arises in the act of forgiveness: I will the perpetrator to be free — free of giving me anything — and I desire what is best for that person, namely, his or her ultimate good.*

But why is it that I am actually able to forgo the validation I so deeply crave?

Because I do not need it.

I am able to forgo validation from my perpetrator because I have received validation in a more interior and intimate way. And this intimate affirmation of my being arises in the act of forgiveness: *I will* the perpetrator *to be free* — free of giving me anything — and I desire what is best for that person, namely, his or her ultimate good. To desire this is supremely liberating and can even be emotionally exhilarating. It can also be emotionally exhausting. But either way, as the feelings diminish, at the most fundamental level I release myself from the need for the perpetrator's validation of me, and I release the offender from that indebtedness to me. I experience a type of closure that allows me to move on. This initial sense of closure does not mean the closure can't deepen, as we will discuss later. But the tide is turning. The sun is now closer to setting on my pain than rising. The open wound is now healing.

Joshua's Story

Joshua was thirty-two and a mechanical engineer with a promising future, successfully employed at a leading aerospace company.* He had married while in graduate school. He and Amy, a hygienist and part-time nutritionist, had five-year-old twin girls, and child number three was on the way. Life was good — except that, in some deep place inside Josh, it wasn't.

When Joshua was seventeen, during his junior year in high school, his father dropped dead of a heart attack while playing at a charity golf tournament. Nearly fifteen years later, Joshua began wondering about his deep discontent in life, his defeatism, his sense that he was never good enough — in spite of his many successes, including leading his varsity basketball team to the state

---

*Unless otherwise indicated, throughout the work, individuals referred to in the examples are either fictitious (although based on the clinical and pastoral experiences of the authors and all identifying information has been removed or changed) or under a pseudonym have granted permission for their stories to be used.

championship in his senior year, and receiving a full academic scholarship to MIT. "I just wanted to make Dad proud," he found himself reflecting one day. Yet during his childhood and teen years, *that* — pleasing his father — seemed to be an unattainable dream. "All I could do was never enough. It was never good enough," he thought — a realization that he turned over and over in his mind.

A two-term state senator who ended up with an extremely successful and lucrative law practice, Joshua's father was removed from the family life Joshua lived with his mom, two sisters, and younger brother. As the oldest child, and a male, Joshua never knew a time in childhood when enormous expectations were not riding on his shoulders.

Something he had read led him to wonder if his current state — which was beginning to worry his wife and cause tension in their marriage — was not somehow connected to his relationship with his father. In his early thirties, and after several sessions of therapy with a Catholic psychologist, Joshua discovered that this was indeed the case. Therapy had helped him get down to a deep place of sadness inside himself: He never remembered his dad hugging him or showing him affection. He never saw pleasure in his father's eyes at any accomplishment: No grade, no medal, was ever good enough.

Joshua was able to realize that this wound — a "father wound" — was deep. He also realized that he was deeply, deeply angry at his father. This, in turn, explained why he hadn't shed a tear at his father's funeral Mass, and had seemed then, and for months afterward, enveloped in numbness, bereft of any feeling.

One day at the end of a session, he came to a major breakthrough: He realized he was also angry at his father for dying the way he did. It was almost as if Joshua felt further invalidated by his dad's departure. Oddly, and deep down inside himself somewhere, the teenage Joshua was feeling that he had failed his dad so completely in life that his father just up and left him.

One day Joshua's therapist asked him point blank: "You think maybe you need to forgive your dad?" That was the answer — Joshua knew it immediately. But how? How to forgive *all that*? And in a way, Joshua thought, what would it matter? He's dead. Can I forgive a dead man?

What about Saying "I Forgive You"?

There can be times where seeking reconciliation is not prudent or is, for other reasons, impossible.

As we've seen, an apology from the perpetrator is not a prerequisite for obtaining the freedom of forgiveness. Yet in spite of this reality, we can find ourselves feeling, as Josh did, that we need to do something more. We wonder whether verbalizing the forgiveness — "I forgive you" — is necessary or appropriate. Or perhaps we feel compelled to tell the perpetrator those words, perhaps even as a measure of the justice that is due to us: Whether he wants to hear those words or not, my own dignity requires me, so it seems, to say those words to his face. Or maybe we just wonder — like Joshua — whether our forgiveness can be real if we don't say those words. Oftentimes, we might feel moved, upon forgiving the offender, to seek a quick reconciliation with him or her. Yet, there can be times where seeking reconciliation is not prudent or is, for other reasons, impossible.

We'll have more to say in chapter 9 about saying "I forgive you," and about the possibilities of reconciling with those who have offended us. Suffice it to say, for now, that the prospect of moving from the interior act of forgiveness to the external expression of that forgiveness — in words, in a handshake, in an embrace — is often a compelling and desirable prospect. Such gestures can serve remarkably to confirm and reinforce, audibly and visibly, that the interior act has taken place, that it's real. Nonetheless, such expressions are not essential for forgiveness to be real.

Forgiving His Dead Father

Could Joshua somehow reconcile with his dad? Could he speak to him those words — "I forgive you" — even though his father was dead? Such were the questions Joshua wrestled with as he tried to move forward. After several more therapy sessions, Joshua was able to take advantage of a family weekend getaway to wander off into the woods by himself for a couple of hours. He brought with him a journal he had kept since his sophomore year in high school. He came to a bluff overlooking a spring-fed reservoir and, after looking out over the water for a long time, he sat and opened the journal. On a blank page he wrote that day's date and, below it, the words: "I forgive my father — for never being satisfied with me, for never showing me affection, for leaving me." And he ended with, "Dad, I forgive you — for everything."

Although he couldn't say those words in person, he believed and prayed that his father could hear them. What had triggered this possibility? Some weeks earlier, after opening up to his elderly mother about all this, she had confided: "Josh, your dad was emotionally distant — he was that way with all you kids and even with me. What you never knew was that I became pregnant before we were married. We were already engaged, but your father and I felt we weren't ready for a baby when we were so young. So I had an abortion. Shortly after, we were both heartbroken. We struggled to accept that we had done what we had done.

"Even though we repented, your father, deep down, could

never forgive himself. He could never get over it. He felt he was a failure as a father. He struggled all our married life to be successful at something — even though he knew that success as a father was beyond him. Somehow, by his political and legal careers, he tried to provide for us — his poor way of showing love. I'm sorry I didn't tell you this years ago."

As Joshua listened to his mother, he was overcome with empathy — a profound sense of pity — for his dad. He hugged his mom and then burst into tears on her shoulder, something he had never done before. He now was in a place where he could let go of all the hurt, disappointment, and sadness. Joshua had never heard his father tell him: "I love you." Joshua was never able to tell his father during his life on earth: "I forgive you." Yet without ever being able to tell this to his father face to face, Joshua was nonetheless able to forgive him. And he was free.

～

Because forgiveness in and of itself is an act of the will, even if I were alone on a desert island, I could still forgive. I could forgive those who, as it turns out, are responsible for the circumstances that landed me on a desert island. I can forgive someone I will never see again. And as we just saw in Joshua's case, I can forgive someone who is dead.

Forgiveness is a supremely free and freeing act of the will. *How* exactly I get to that place where I am able to forgive, to *commit* forgiveness — this is a topic we will explore ahead. As we hope to explain (spoiler alert), we can't commit Christian forgiveness without grace. But in the next chapter, we will consider a much more challenging prospect: How do I forgive myself?

For Reflection and Prayer

1. This chapter explains some of the many misconceptions regarding forgiveness: letting someone off the hook; pretending that the offense didn't happen; pretending that it did not
hurt us; and the idea that we should just forgive and forget.
Did you ever get caught in a trap like one of these? Did you
ever adopt one of these misconceptions and assert that you
had forgiven someone … when you had not?

2. Joshua's story raises many points. What is there about his
journey that stirs your heart? One part of his story is very
common: the need to forgive someone who is not present or
who has died. Consider a person in your life who has already
passed, yet whom you feel the need to forgive. How does
Joshua's story impact you?

Chapter 2
Maybe the Hardest Case of All

What Does It Mean to Forgive Yourself?

I think that if God forgives us, we must forgive ourselves.
Otherwise, it is almost like setting up
ourselves as a higher tribunal than Him.

— *C. S. Lewis to a Lady, April 19, 1951*

While we can muster the strength to cancel another's debt to us, we might find the prospect of applying a similar mercy to ourselves unthinkable. In fact, some Christians ask whether the very concept of self-forgiveness is inherently problematic or contradictory. Or even whether self-forgiveness is a theologically valid notion in light of the surpassing power of grace that floods our spirit when we receive God's forgiveness.[1]

The rationale goes like this: If you apologize, or at least tell God that you are sorry — and particularly in the Sacrament of Reconciliation — then the Lord forgives you. If the Lord forgives you, if you have received forgiveness from the One who made heaven and earth, then you have no need for your pitiful, relatively minuscule self-forgiveness. Simply accept the Lord's forgiveness and you will be free: "So if the Son sets you free, you really will be free" (Jn 8:36, NASB). In fact, the anti-self-forgiveness perspective claims that the failure to forgive or accept yourself after receiving the Lord's forgiveness indicates a narcissistic tendency, a lack of faith and trust in God, or worse.

Yet this seems to be at odds with our human experience and, in some sense, with our human nature. Just ask any therapist or any Catholic priest who regularly hears confessions. We'll tell you that one of the most frequent struggles, even of committed and well-formed Catholics, is the struggle to forgive oneself: "Father, how do I forgive myself?" "I know I've been forgiven, but I can't get past this, I can't let go of the shame."[2]

Our contention, based on ample clinical and pastoral experience, is that there is indeed something to self-forgiveness that is normal, natural, and not narcissistic. And while it is a work of grace, founded on our Lord's forgiveness, self-forgiveness nonetheless stands humanly and psychologically as a particular and crucial kind of action in its own right, distinct both from receiving forgiveness (human or divine) and from forgiving another.

Self-Forgiveness: Is It a Valid Concept?

To begin with, just as in forgiving someone else, forgiving yourself is not letting yourself off the hook. It's not condoning evil. It's not saying what you did was OK. It's not excusing yourself or removing responsibility from yourself. There are certainly invalid and problematic interpretations of self-forgiveness, just as there are faulty and inauthentic concepts of forgiveness.

Forgiving yourself, as we will see, is different in nature from forgiving someone else — and might well be susceptible to other names. As we hope to show, self-forgiveness is a much more fluid concept than that of forgiving another. We will here nonetheless employ the term "self-forgiveness" given its ubiquitous use and immediate comprehension.

Next, and without getting too philosophical, we might just consider whether the very notion of self-forgiveness is valid, at least at face value, by asking whether the notion of self-*anything* is valid. In our everyday experience of ourselves, we meaningfully refer to all kinds of reflexive actions that we engage in with regard to ourselves. We are self-conscious. We are self-aware. We self-medicate, self-examine, and engage in self-care. We can be self-accepting or self-loathing. We claim a capacity for self-knowledge and self-understanding. We can experience self-compassion, we can commit acts of self-injury, and we can experience self-hatred.

Well-adjusted and emotionally mature individuals are said to be able to objectify their emotions, experiences, and perceptions, putting a kind of "space" between self and emotions in order to examine and assess what they are experiencing. We reflect on our personal growth. We look back on our own personal history. We consider memories, desires, achievements, dreams, thought patterns, imaginations, trauma, feelings, bodily changes, emotions, mood swings, spiritual growth, and more. A well-adjusted and emotionally mature person is able to participate in this type of self-reflection.

Take as another example one of the most often addressed phenomena in counseling today: self-talk. "Self-talk" is the running narrative or inner monologue that typically accompanies us throughout the day. We constantly weave together narratives about what is happening to us. At the heart of mental and spiritual health is the need to realize the power of those narratives, and objectify, verify, or correct certain elements. Healthy individuals pay attention to their self-talk, but are able to step back and analyze it and even modify it, as needed.

In a word, we are very peculiar animals in that we have this marvelous capacity for self-reflection and for reflexive actions upon ourselves.[3]

So granting all this and the myriad behaviors — both positive and negative — that we direct at ourselves, surely we can also direct forgiveness at ourselves. In this, self-forgiveness is indeed a valid and very meaningful concept.

In fact, self-forgiveness corresponds to a deep kind of healing that we often need through life. That's why later on in this book we will explore how to ask God for the grace of genuine self-forgiveness. And, as we will now explore, self-forgiveness is deeply connected to self-talk, to the narrative we construct about ourselves, and to an extremely powerful emotion that all of us deal with throughout life: shame.

Understanding Self-Forgiveness in Light of the Universal Experience of Shame

Is self-forgiveness similar to forgiving another person? Normally when I forgive another, as we saw in chapter 1, I forgo the need for validation in light of a newfound sense of self-worth and interior freedom, which, in a sense, is profoundly self-validating. Forgiving ourselves, like forgiveness in general, involves a letting go, the surrendering of something that we very deeply sense that we need. In forgiving others, we let go of our need for validation. In forgiving ourselves, a similar yet distinct dynamic occurs: We let go of the need to punish ourselves. In order to understand this better, it will help to reflect on the universal human experience of the emotion we call shame.[4] First, allow us to talk briefly about emotions in general.

Emotions are reactions that we have that tell us something about us and our environment. Sometimes the emotional reaction is a perfect reflection of the environment, and sometimes it is simply melodramatic. Said another way, sometimes the emotional reactions are accurate and sometimes they are inaccurate.[5]

Forgiving ourselves, like forgiveness in general, involves a letting go, the surrendering of something that we very deeply sense that we need. In forgiving others, we let go of our need for validation.

Most researchers are quick to note the distinction between the emotions of shame and guilt, noting as well that neither emotion is entirely negative: Both guilt and shame can be appropriate reactions and necessary building blocks of our personality. Guilt accompanies the conviction that "I did something bad." This is good and helpful. Shame, however, has a radically different focus: not the bad choice or action, but the actor — *me*. Shame says, "*I* am bad." We typically think of shame as a negative and unhelpful emotion — and that is largely the case. But we would be remiss if we did not briefly note that, like guilt, shame sometimes has a positive side. Let the psychologist explain.

I (Dr. Lock) have always been small in stature. Standing today at five foot two, I'm often the shortest guy in the room. On top of that, I acknowledge that I've never been able to reliably shoot a basket. What would happen if, not realizing my limits, I were to go out on the basketball court with professionals? I'd rightly feel a certain amount of shame — feeling that "I am bad" for entering a place where I don't belong. I'd have the feeling that I'm lacking, that I'm incompetent, that I'm doing something wrong. And that would be true! I'd also feel fear, but that's another story. With all seriousness, the feeling of shame can help to hold us back — to help us remain humble and accepting of our limitations. So shame can be good and helpful.

But shame can also be destructive and wicked.

Remember, emotions are reactions that tell us something about ourselves and our environment — sometimes accurate and sometimes inaccurate. Shame, focusing on the actor — me — often says that "I am bad." Frequently, that's not only inaccurate, but destructive. But we all carry that message around with us to some degree. Throughout our lives, it might take on different nuances: "I'm not good enough"; "I'll fail"; "I don't fit in"; "I'm not worthy"; "I'm not lovable." Like tar stuck to our fingers, shame is always there trying to influence our self-understanding.

Shame is fed not only by our objectively bad choices and behaviors, but also by the emotional traumas to which we are subjected.[6]

Ed's Story

Ed and Emily were happily married for forty-eight years. On her birthday, Emily suffered a massive stroke. She briefly regained consciousness while in the ICU for over two weeks and was able to communicate by blinking her eyelids, but complications set in, and she died.

Weeks after her passing, and still in the throes of mourning, Ed was struggling to understand what had happened. The ICU physician explained to him that her death likely resulted from atrial fibrillation — AFib — the most common form of arrhythmia or irregular heartbeat. Ed had never heard of AFib, but when the doctor questioned Ed about whether he had ever noticed some typical symptoms in Emily, Ed realized in hindsight that he had. Those symptoms include fatigue and shortness of breath. Ed remembered that Emily had complained occasionally about both symptoms over the previous year or so, but he had chalked it up to old age. While he had commented in passing that Emily should get a checkup, he didn't insist, and Emily wasn't an alarmist — she, too, thought it was simply old age.

Ed also recalled one occasion when she forgot something they had talked about over breakfast that very morning. When he brought the topic up at lunch time, she couldn't remember discussing it. He shared this with the doctor, who helped Ed realize, in hindsight, that Emily likely suffered a transient ischemic episode, a precursor of what would be the fatal stroke.

Not only was Ed heartbroken and in profound grief, he was grappling with an overwhelming sense of failure. He couldn't undo the consequences of his failure to act more attentively and carefully with Emily. It was too late to correct his assessment that Emily was simply experiencing age-related decline. He was assailed by merciless and piercing self-blame: How could he not have seen? How could he not have been more concerned? How could he not have made her go to the doctor? Ed felt lost and, worst of all, he felt condemned to end his life in a dark place of self-loathing.

Ed even went to confession and asked the priest to absolve

him for what he did to Emily. The priest assured Ed that he had not sinned, he was simply unaware of the warning signs. Ed dismissed that explanation and insisted, "I should have known!" Ed asked the priest to give him absolution and the priest complied. Still, nothing seemed to change. Ed could never forgive himself for what he had failed to do.

Shame and Self-Punishment

We'll return to Ed in a moment, but his story so far will help us to understand how shame can weave its way into our life. When over the years our traumas, big and little, have all had their cumulative effect and we have internalized shame's message ("I am bad"), the results can be overwhelming. To relieve the internal tension of shame, we often self-medicate: shopping, working, gambling, abusing alcohol, using drugs, using porn, through masturbation, and the list goes on. Yet — and this might come as a surprise — often our preferred method is to punish ourselves.

To be sure, most of us over time become secret experts at punishing ourselves. It's actually far, far more common than we might think, as attested to by the psychological couch and the confessional box. And we're not talking about the section of the population that is mentally ill. It's the general population — it's all of us.

On a purely psychological level, self-punishment is a way of temporarily reducing the emotional pain of guilt and shame. Self-loathing, self-degradation, and other forms of self-mistreatment are all manifestations of self-punishment. Somehow, often very early in life, we learn that meting out hurt to ourselves relieves guilt — at least temporarily. But this dynamic also traps us in a vicious and unhealthy cycle of behavior. Since self-punishment never staunches the shame completely, we apply more self-punishment, and the cycle continues. And we can go on for years cycling through shame and self-punishment, becoming so habituated to it that we lose awareness, and the cycle becomes submerged in our psyche — often manifesting itself in neurotic behaviors.

The person trapped in shame engages in behaviors subconsciously aimed at relieving the emotional turmoil of shame, but that only end up drawing the individual more deeply into the shame.

It's like sinking in quicksand.

When we give free reign to shame, we acquire a false sense of resolution. Resolving that "I'm just a bad person" brings a kind of deceptive validation to my turmoil. It seems — though incorrectly — that I am dealing with my turmoil, indeed that I am accepting something about myself. This elicits a false sense of closure to my problem not unlike the times when, as adolescents, we quit track, didn't try out for the drama club, or didn't ask a girl out because "I'm not good enough." That negative emotion brought closure to — and in some sense, relief from — the inner turmoil of: "I don't think I'm good enough ... but I want to try ... but what if I fail?"

Shame tricks us into believing the matter is now closed. Much like giving up on trying to free myself from the quicksand, there might be a certain odd, paradoxical, and fleeting sense of closure and resolution to the dire situation: "I give up. I can't get out. I'm just going to die from heat exhaustion and exposure. There's nothing I can do about it." That same dynamic of shame is intensified when I rest in an unwillingness to forgive myself. This unwillingness engenders a false, and transitory, sense of closure to my inner turmoil, though the turmoil, in fact, will not leave me. Those people seemingly stuck in self-condemnation are actually attempting (and failing) to relieve themselves from the emotional turmoil of shame. In short: Resting in and repeating the belief that "I'm a bad person" gives the semblance of relieving that inner turmoil but ultimately does not.

This is very different from the true sense of resolution in which a proportionate and healthy sense of shame for choices I have made — perhaps some very bad choices — moves me, not to despair, but to genuine repentance and reform of life. Rather than allowing shame to overpower me with the conviction that I am bad, I recognize that things I have done are bad. I admit, I apologize, I repent, I am willing to accept the consequences for my bad choices, I seek reconciliation and to amend my life. Perhaps I have committed sins that warrant hell, but I have sought the Lord's forgiveness and received it. And he sees my goodness and affirms me in his love.

As with forgiveness in all other cases, self-forgiveness takes an act of the will.

The unwillingness to forgive myself, quite to the contrary, is experienced as an entrapment in — and an acute and suffocating intensification of — the belief that "I am not good." Remaining in the state of self-unforgiveness gives the impression that the scales have been balanced: I'm bad, I did something bad, the only way to even come close to making this right is for me to remain in this state of self-punishment. I tell myself that this is the only way my future can be written.

Self-Forgiveness and the Art of Escaping Quicksand

What does it mean to forgive myself? Rather than simply arrive at a definition of self-forgiveness, we prefer to pursue our analogy of quicksand to explain it: Forgiving myself is like freeing myself from quicksand. Both are processes, and both are tricky.

Forgiving ourselves involves first and foremost the choice to stop punishing ourselves. As with forgiveness in all other cases, self-forgiveness takes an act of the will.

The choice to stop punishing ourselves requires that we step out of the process by which we succumb to shame. We begin by interrupting that process of giving in to our feeling of shame, a process that only leads us to sink deeper in it. We work steadily and patiently to first get one leg free from the quicksand of shame, then the other, crawling and dragging ourselves out of shame's dynamic.

This can be accomplished by two self-interventions, one cognitively focused and one emotionally. In the cognitive interventions, we interrupt the self-destructive thinking — "I'm not a good person … I can't forgive myself" — that only offers a false and fleeting sense of resolution to my inner turmoil.

In the emotional intervention, we enter the experience of the positive self-statement — "I forgive myself" — and allow ourselves to feel the emotions that well up as we take this healthy truth deeper into our hearts. We might then take further steps emotionally, such as making a detailed distinction between the fact that we aren't good at one task, but at our core we are good — and then sitting with the feelings that statement evokes. Yet another emotional approach to pulling yourself out of the quicksand of shame is to embrace the accurate negative self-assessment: "I'm sometimes far less than perfect and so sometimes my behavior is bad, but I'm trying" — and then allowing yourself to experience the grief of not living up to your reputation as you have concocted it in your own mind.

Experiencing and accepting the emotions that come will help the grieving to progress. And as we grieve and feel our feelings, as the painful feelings dissipate — as the mist clears — we see reality. We can then make an accurate assessment of ourselves, and in the process lose the desire for self-punishment.

Ed's Story Revisited

Ed couldn't see beyond himself and his failures. His emotional state shifted from grief at the loss of his wife to self-hatred at his failure to realize the medical episodes that she suffered. A friend reached out to Ed a few months after the funeral and was shocked to find Ed sounding even more grief-stricken than he was at the funeral. The friend, out of concern, said, "Ed, this is so sad, but it wasn't your fault. You really have to forgive yourself." Something in his friend's words resonated within him, even if ever so slightly.

So Ed returned to his confessor to ask how he could ever forgive himself. The priest asked Ed to tell his full story and recount all the ways in which he felt he had failed. This was an emotional experience for Ed as he not only recalled the events of Emily's last days and all the signs he ignored, but also as he recalled similar situations in his life.

It turns out that Ed's inability to forgive himself was embedded in a generalized web of unforgiveness of others. And he realized that the failure to forgive himself affected other areas of his relationship with Emily.

Ed also came to see that beyond forgiving himself, he had to forgive his wife for not recognizing the signs in herself, not only for this situation, but also for many similar situations where Emily had under-reacted. Further, Ed also realized that he resented Emily's friends for their failure to see the signs in Emily.

Finally Ed realized that he was angry with God. He thought it was unfair of the Lord to make the signs of Emily's illness so vague — even when Ed saw the signs, he couldn't interpret them. It seemed to him that God was cruel. As Ed shared these details, he felt a burden lifting. He could see more clearly how the event unfolded, and he began to internalize the sense that he really didn't know what was happening. Certainly, if he had known, he would have taken action.

Finally Ed decided he wanted to forgive himself. He also felt a sense of compassion for Emily and for her friends. The priest then led Ed through deep-seated acts of forgiveness for each one of these circumstances and persons involved. Ultimately, Ed was able to accept that his failure was partly because of his tendency to avoid situations that scared him and partly because of his ignorance of medical disorders. As a result of this exercise, he ultimately replaced his self-condemnation with the honest and realistic statement, "I did the best I could."

~

To forgive ourselves is to short-circuit and break the vicious circle of futile self-punishment. This involves creating a reflective distance between myself and the narrative that shame is fueling within me. This requires an act of will to renounce self-punishment as a response to shame. As Curt Thompson explains: "The very act of recognizing shame means that we stop and shift our attention in such a way that we interrupt our progression down the shame trail. In so doing we give ourselves the opportunity to chart a different course."[7]

In forgiving myself, I muster the courage to consider a new narrative. Writing that new narrative, and not allowing shame to direct the narrative, requires time, acts of graced imagination, the processing of emotions, and the support of true friends who, as Thompson later emphasizes, can reinforce our conviction that we are loved and that our shame is to be dismissed. The mission of that community is to call us to "new life." There we can receive the empathy we need to risk trusting "a newly imagined story, one of healing, redemption and joy." Here we can learn "not only a way to forgive the past but also to create a new future."[8]

For Reflection and Prayer

1. To a greater or lesser extent, we all struggle with shame for certain actions, thoughts, behaviors, and so forth. Ask the Holy Spirit to guide your thinking as you examine your own life. Consider writing down those incidents or thought processes that are holding you back from forgiving yourself. Then bring them one by one to prayer and, if appropriate, to the sacrament of confession. If you are finding the process stressful, consider asking a counselor or priest to guide you.

2. Identify friends who can support you as you begin the journey of self-forgiveness, people who can reinforce the reality that you are loved. How might you tell them that you are beginning this healing journey and would welcome their support and prayers? This is especially important if you are dealing with major wounds that have led you to self-punish.

Chapter 3
How Do You Know When You've Really Forgiven Someone?

Human Forgiveness and Graced Forgiveness

So let us confidently approach the throne of grace to receive mercy and to find grace for timely help.

— Hebrews 4:16

51

To the extent that we've already lived a good portion of life fighting the good fight of forgiveness, sooner or later we get the sense that forgiving is not a uniform or one-off kind of thing (at least most of the time). At times we wonder whether we've really forgiven this person ... or not. If I forgave him, why am I not over it? Maybe I really haven't forgiven. Or maybe my forgiveness was incomplete. And — what is real forgiveness anyway?

Is There Such a Thing as Complete Forgiveness?

Both authors can attest — one of us as a confessor, the other as a therapist — that forgiveness happens along a continuum. And that fact is borne out because arriving at, and remaining in, a place of forgiveness is hard work. Really hard work! It can feel like scaling a rock wall and getting to a certain location on the rock face that you were determined to get to, but then having to exert all kinds of effort to stay there. As we will see in a later chapter, our initial act of forgiveness, depending on the situation, might require *renewal* from time to time in order to persist in our hearts.

This is why at times our initial forays into that uncharted territory of forgiveness might only seem partial; and perhaps in some real sense the initial attempt *is* only partial due to underlying conditions we have perhaps unconsciously placed on the forgiveness. The nature of forgiveness is such that it allows for deeper and deeper exercises, richer and more incisive acts of forgiveness that proceed from deeper and deeper recesses of the will and our openness to grace.

So here's a perhaps startling proposition: Any given act of forgiveness might never be "complete," "full," or "perfect" — at least in this life. And that's OK. What we're aiming for most of the time is an act of forgiveness that is sufficient for now, or is as complete as I am currently able, with God's grace, to render for now.

Here's why. To use a sporting analogy, forgiveness is like a backswing in tennis. After years of practice, some swings become spectacular, others are still lacking. But a backswing is never actually perfect or complete, not even for a pro. All human arts and creations are always open to greater perfection. Does a parent ever master the art of parenting *completely*? Is any work of art, however famous or conceivably perfect, not open to further perfection? Ask an artist and they will tell you: They are never done with their creation. Instead of it being complete or done, they are finished ... for now.

This also seems to be the nature of human forgiveness, even when elevated and transformed by grace, a topic we will explore just ahead. When we forgive another in Christ, enabled by his power, we are given the wonderful possibility of reflecting the omnipotence, the unlimited power, of the Creator in forgiving and thereby healing his creature. Yet this always happens, in our case, within the limitations of being human. So human forgiveness, even aided by grace, is always open to further perfection. We can forgive others, all the while sensing that we will need to renew that act of forgiveness, that it is open to better and deeper expression. This is a topic we'll explore in chapter 6.

As for *complete* forgiveness, only God's forgiveness could ever meaningfully be called *complete*:

> Who is a God like you, who removes guilt / and pardons sin for the remnant of his inheritance; / Who does not persist in anger forever,

> *Any given act of forgiveness might never be "complete," "full," or "perfect"— at least in this life. And that's OK.*

/ but instead delights in mercy, / And will again have compassion on us, treading underfoot our iniquities? / You will cast into the depths of the sea all our sins. (Micah 7:18–19)

When God forgives, it is final. There is no perfecting it. The completeness and absoluteness of his forgiveness is a demonstration of his omnipotence — omnipotence in his magnificent mercy. And here it is wonderful to remember that, while we are able to forgive *yet not forget*, our amazing and merciful God, once we have repented of our sins and he has forgiven us, *no longer takes them into any account*. Sacred Scripture affirms time and again that God destroys the memory of our sinfulness: "None of the crimes he has committed shall be remembered against him" (Ez 18:22); "Peace in place of bitterness! / You have preserved my life / from the pit of destruction; / Behind your back / you cast all my sins" (Is 38:17); "Repent, therefore, and be converted, that your sins may be wiped away, and that the Lord may grant you times of refreshment" (Acts 3:19–20). It's as if God takes on a holy amnesia out of love for us. And having forgiven us, God treats us — as in the case of the prodigal son — as if those sins had never happened.[1]

Is There Such a Thing as Partial Forgiveness?

Just because I sense that my act of forgiveness is difficult, of poor quality, and that I'm really struggling to remain in a place of forgiveness, it does not mean the forgiveness is not real. As we just saw, it means that at the very least my act of forgiveness is open to further perfection. It might also mean that my forgiveness is actually partial in some sense.

But is there such a thing as partial forgiveness? Partial forgiveness can be a state where we would like to forgive, but we have a hard time saying, "I have forgiven as completely as I possibly can" because we have the sense that we are not "there" yet. It might make sense to talk about forgiveness being partial in a scenario where the offense to be forgiven is actually made up of multiple parts. For example, Dale's cousin Evan never paid back the two thousand dollars Dale lent him — never owning up to his default on the loan, but actually concocting an elaborate story (one Dale knew to be false) about how Evan needed to use that money to assist his mom who had become unexpectedly unemployed and could not pay her rent.

Dale happens to know Evan has a gambling habit — *and* his own mother, Dale's aunt, confided to Dale that Evan never actually covered her rent money. Dale can forgive him for caving in to his gambling habit (and he probably tells himself that he should have known better when he lent Evan the money in the first place), but he struggles to forgive Evan for lying through his teeth. Dale's forgiveness is partial.

And it's partial because life is messy. Back in the Garden of Eden before the Fall, Adam and Eve lived an amazing life. They did not yet have the effects of original sin, so they were able to experience a type of personal integration that we all long for. They didn't have an internal battle over the decision to have dessert or not. They were able to navigate tough decisions with a certain harmony between their emotions and intellect, in unison. After the Fall, this was not so.

The effects of original sin have left us with a certain disunity within ourselves, and we often feel a lack of integration in our actions. The harmony is off by a few notes. Just as we crave the richness of different notes working together in harmony, so too we crave the richness of fully integrated actions. We sense a certain dissonance within us if we find ourselves in Dale's shoes. We want to forgive Evan for everything, but part of our messy world is that certain things will be more difficult for us to forgive. And that's OK. Our Lord loves our honesty. He loves our humility when we are willing to admit the messiness and the struggle.

Premature Forgiveness and False Forgiveness

There can be other instances in which the forgiveness is partial because it is premature. We might feel that we've "kind of" forgiven. When we find ourselves feeling this way, it might be the case that we haven't quite arrived at a genuine act of forgiveness. In fact, we would suggest that the sense of having "kind of" forgiven someone, more often than not, simply reflects the fact that we are still struggling to forgive; that genuine forgiveness might not have actually happened yet.

Christian forgiveness does not require that we steamroll our own sense of respect for ourselves.

In assisting people who grapple with forgiveness in their lives, both of us have often heard them explain how, even though they continue to struggle with forgiveness, they forgave their perpetrators "immediately" and "without a doubt in my mind" because "I just had to." And we might well ask: Isn't that the Christian thing to do? Or maybe we were raised in strict Catholic homes where we had it pounded into us: "Forgive and forget — that's what God expects of you!" We're compelled to think that if we don't forgive immediately, we'll be sinning. (How can you pray the Our Father without forgiving, right?) This is called premature forgiveness because we have not really entered into the choice for forgiveness.

When forgiveness is — presumably — granted with little or no consideration for oneself, sometimes in a knee-jerk fashion, we would have to wonder about the genuineness of that forgiveness. Christian forgiveness does not require that we steamroll our own sense of self-respect. As we will see in a later chapter, in cases of deeply malicious and criminal harms, forgiveness is not opposed to seeking that the perpetrator be brought to justice.

Whether the harms are big or small, knee-jerk forgiveness should always be examined more deeply. Not surprisingly, people in such situations can find themselves wondering after a time whether they actually forgave or not. What might have happened — passing for forgiveness — was that they reacted with mere sentimentalism, an overprizing of "feeling." It doesn't feel good to be in a place of resentment, anger, and hurt, and so we quickly try to neutralize the bad feelings by "forgiving." An extreme example of this would be a hostage succumbing to the Stockholm Syndrome: He acquires a feeling of trust and affection ("forgiveness") toward his captors. Another extreme example would be the unfortunate young woman, stuck in a toxic relationship, who repeatedly "forgives" the man who cyclically abuses her physically and emotionally.

In such instances, we're not really talking about forgiveness at all, but rather about a kind of false or pseudoforgiveness which can take many forms. Perhaps Dale has "forgiven" Evan as a way of self-medicating or coping with the guilt that he feels toward Evan — as might happen if he were quietly having an affair with Evan's wife.

False forgiveness can also be at work when the supposed forgiveness is still seeking vengeance, when I still want to harm the offender. Your motto here might be: "Forgive — but retaliate!" Another version of this is when we say, "I would forgive him, but first he needs to admit that he was wrong." Genuine forgiveness leaves no room for retaliation or conditions.

As we will explore in later chapters, while anger toward the offender can be natural and even healthy, hatred is not. Forgiveness means getting to a place where we genuinely desire every good thing for the offender — which is not opposed to seeking that the perpetrator of grave harm be brought to justice. Genuine forgiveness seeks justice, not vengeance.

It can also happen that our ego gets involved: I hold myself to be so virtuous that "of course" I forgive this person. Haven't we all done that at some point in our lives? Yet this quick forgiving might be little more than a manifestation of a false humility and a subtle form of pride. We want to look good or feel good, so we say we forgive, even though we harbor deep and unexamined unforgiveness, sadness, and anger.

Such unexamined forgiveness is too often an attempt to remain blissfully ignorant of the true and profound ways that we have been hurt. Premature forgiveness is a way to avoid the pain and make it all better by proclaiming words that sound good to us, perhaps even churchy or holy, but which are in fact hollow.

Human Forgiveness and Graced Forgiveness

So the forgiveness that we seem to feel capable of, on a human level, is always open to perfecting, to deepening, to renewal. And no doubt one can very validly look at forgiveness as an entirely human phenomenon. Forgiveness is not, of itself, something reserved only for Christians, as we have already noted. For many millennia, even before the coming of Christ, human beings have been engaging in forgiveness in different forms and with varying degrees of depth, reflected in such terms as: "pardon," "pity," "acquittal," "remission," and so on.

Jesus acknowledged the *human* phenomenon of forgiveness. For example, in his parable of the unforgiving servant, the servant's master initially pardons his debt: "Moved with compassion the master of that servant let him go and forgave him the loan" (Mt 18:27). Jesus recognized that on a merely human level, some form of forgiveness was possible.

In our day, forgiveness, with its full-throated involvement of one human person and another — its interpersonal dimension — and all the human toll it exacts at times, and the messiness of it all, is not in itself an experience exclusive to the baptized. Many a thoroughly secular, non-practicing, agnostic humanitarian could share stories of gut-wrenching forgiveness in their lives — imparted and received. And their forgiveness is quite real and quite profound.

So does grace make a difference? Is there a difference between the kind of forgiveness the agnostic can engage in and the kind of forgiveness the committed Christian can engage in?

Yes. And it can make a dramatic difference.

The medieval adage was true: *Grace builds on nature.* Through baptism, believers become enlivened with the gift of supernatural charity. We are elevated by grace to love with a more-than-human love, to love with the love of God himself, to love with a flame of the love in the heart of Jesus. The first Greek-speaking Christians called this novelty, this new expression of love, *agape.*

Agape-love is divinely infused love — infused directly into our souls. It is the gift of giving ourselves in some measure as God freely gives himself to and for us. It is giving without expecting anything in return. It is the love fully manifested in Jesus Christ. And agape-love *is what makes the difference between human forgiveness and forgiveness elevated by grace.* Graced forgiveness is human forgiveness infused, energized, elevated with the divine dynamism of agape-love.[2]

This is the very wondrous transformation that C. S. Lewis relished in *The Four Loves*, his exploration of how divinely infused charity — agape-love — can and is meant to transform the human forms of love, namely, family love, friendship, and romantic love or *eros*. Writes Lewis:

> Divine Love does not substitute itself for the natural —
> as if we had to throw away our silver to make room for
> the gold. The natural loves are summoned to become
> modes of Charity while also remaining the natural loves
> they were.
>
> One sees here at once a sort of echo or rhyme or
> corollary to the Incarnation itself. And this need not
> surprise us, for the Author of both is the same. As Christ
> is perfect God and perfect Man, the natural loves are
> called to become perfect Charity and also perfect nat-
> ural loves.
>
> As God becomes Man "not by conversion of the
> Godhead into flesh, but by taking of the Manhood into
> God", so here; Charity does not dwindle into merely
> natural love but natural love is taken up into, made the
> tuned and obedient instrument of, Love Himself.

Grace can elevate and perfect human forgiveness while that forgiveness remains quite itself. We should not be surprised, then, that at times we might not be able to distinguish human forgiveness from graced forgiveness.

On the other hand, the difference can also be extraordinary.

History is full of the most unspeakable crimes to which victims responded with a dazzling heroic forgiveness, offered in the name of Christ. Moved by the deepest motions of divinely infused charity, they offered the perpetrators of their suffering a forgiveness that boggles the mind. Think, for example, of St. Maximilian Kolbe, wasted to the bone after two weeks in his starvation bunker at Auschwitz, peacefully looking into the face of the SS officer about to inject him with carbolic acid — and serenely offering him his left arm.

So yes, there is a real distinction — and in many ways a quantum leap — between human forgiveness, and genuine Christian forgiveness, forgiveness in Christ, prompted by the Holy Spirit and elevated by charity.

Through his Holy Spirit dwelling in the believer, Jesus can empower us to do as he did, and to live a new kind of life, the life of the "new man" and "new woman" in Christ. We can begin to live a divine life while still on earth. Jesus enables us to do for others what the Father does superabundantly for humanity: to forgive. To be empowered by grace to forgive the brother or sister who has offended me is to accomplish something God-like, something divine.

Jesus enables us to do for others what the Father does superabundantly for humanity: to forgive. To be empowered by grace to forgive the brother or sister who has offended me is to accomplish something God-like.

Just how dramatic the qualitative leap can be from natural human forgiveness to graced forgiveness, *forgiveness in Christ*, and how Jesus can bring this about in our hearts will be the topic of our next chapter.

For Reflection and Prayer

1. Premature forgiveness is something that Christians must

guard against. We know that the "right answer" is to forgive, but often our head and our heart do not move in unison. Consider a time when you were quick to forgive, but you didn't really mean it. Given the topics covered in this chapter, how might you understand your actions?

2. When God forgives, it's final. This is a powerful fact, yet we have a difficult time wrapping our head around that fact. Consider something for which the Lord has forgiven you, and reflect on the reality that this forgiveness from God is final and perfect. How does that make you feel? What impact does this insight have on you right here, right now?

Chapter 4
Opening to Grace

How Jesus Helps Us to Forgive

*So also Christ, offered once to take away the sins of
many, will appear a second time, not to take away sin
but to bring salvation to those who eagerly await him.*

— Hebrews 9:28

Jesus came for the forgiveness of sins. That's a truth at the center of Christian faith. In a nutshell, that was God the Father's plan from all eternity — to save his most beloved creatures from their tragic flaw — original sin. "He delivered us from the power of darkness and transferred us to the kingdom of his beloved

Son, in whom we have redemption, the forgiveness of sins" (Col 1:13–14).[1]

Forgiving sins is something that Jesus does on any number of occasions in the gospels. He forgives the sins of a paralytic man lowered down to him through the ceiling (see Mt 9:2; Mk 2:5; Lk 5:20), and those of a woman who anointed his feet in the home of Simon the Pharisee (Lk 7:47–48). Of course, Scripture is clear that only God can forgive sins; hence the objections of the bystanders:

> Then the scribes and Pharisees began to ask themselves, "Who is this who speaks blasphemies? Who but God alone can forgive sins?" (Lk 5:21)

> The others at table said to themselves, "Who is this who even forgives sins?" (Lk 7:49)

> "Why does this man speak that way? He is blaspheming. Who but God alone can forgive sins?" (Mk 2:7)

What they don't see is that he who speaks, he who forgives, is God.

And then there is John 8:11 — Jesus' encounter with the woman caught in adultery — where we see Jesus speak not only as a man in not condemning the woman, but as God in forgiving her: "Then Jesus said, 'Neither do I condemn you. Go, [and] from now on do not sin any more.'" Jesus the God-man, in every word, every gesture, reveals to us what divine life in us can and should look like. He does so most poignantly in forgiving, be it with the woman caught in adultery, or with his executioners, the "good thief," or even Peter who denied him three times.

Note that there is no holding back in Jesus' forgiveness. He fully forgives. He doesn't partially forgive. He doesn't tell the

woman caught in adultery, "Yeah, you're forgiven and all that …
but I am still so mad at you for sinning!" The response of Jesus is
total. The forgiveness offered is complete.

Jesus Expects His Disciples to Forgive

If the Master forgives, he expects no less from his disciples. In
the Gospel of Matthew, at the heart of Jesus' Sermon on the
Mount, he gives his teaching on prayer. At the conclusion of the
narrative in which Jesus gives us the Lord's Prayer, he continues:
"If you forgive others their transgressions, your heavenly Father
will forgive you. But if you do not forgive others, neither will
your Father forgive your transgressions" (Mt 6:14–15).

And this has a parallel passage in Mark: "When you stand to
pray, forgive anyone against whom you have a grievance, so that
your heavenly Father may in turn forgive you your transgressions" (Mk 11:25–26). In Matthew's Gospel, this follows upon
the petition of the Lord's Prayer in which we ask that he "forgive
us our debts, as we forgive our debtors" (Mt 6:12).

Not surprisingly, we find forgiveness at the heart of St. Paul's
conception of the Christian moral life. He exhorts us:

> Put to death, then, the parts of you that are earthly: im-
> morality, impurity, passion, evil desire, and the greed that
> is idolatry. Because of these the wrath of God is coming
> [upon the disobedient]. By these you too once conduct-
> ed yourselves, when you lived in that way. But now you
> must put them all away: anger, fury, malice, slander, and
> obscene language out of your mouths. Stop lying to one
> another, since you have taken off the old self with its
> practices and have put on the new self, which is being
> renewed, for knowledge, in the image of its creator. Here
> there is not Greek and Jew, circumcision and uncircum-

cision, barbarian, Scythian, slave, free; but Christ is all and in all.

Put on then, as God's chosen ones, holy and beloved, heartfelt compassion, kindness, humility, gentleness, and patience, bearing with one another and *forgiving one another, if one has a grievance against another; as the Lord has forgiven you, so must you also do.* (Colossians 3:5–13, emphasis added)

That new moral behavior includes many expressions, but at its very core is the readiness to forgive others "as the Lord" has forgiven us. Yet Jesus is not simply proposing to his followers that we should follow his example. It's actually deeper than that — much deeper. He proposes that we allow him to give us the capacity and the strength to forgive *as he does*, to forgive others *in him*.

Jesus Empowers His Disciples to Forgive

Through the grace of the Holy Spirit dwelling in us, Jesus empowers us to do as he did, to live the new life in Christ, the divine life we begin to live while still on earth. To open ourselves to the power of grace and to forgive others in Christ is a supreme expression of that life, of the otherworldly in us. Every time we forgive in Christ, it is a foretaste of divine life, the beginning of heaven here on earth.

That the act of forgiving likens us, in some sense, to God was not lost on St. Gregory of Nyssa in the fourth century. Commenting on the fifth petition of the Our Father, "forgive us our debts as we forgive our debtors," he writes:

As our enquiry progresses, it comes to the very peak of virtue; for the words of the prayer outline what sort of a person one should be if one would approach God. Such a one is almost no longer shown in terms of human nature, but, through virtue, is likened to God Himself, so that he seems to be another god, in that he does those things that God alone can do. For the forgiving of debts is the special prerogative of God, since it is said, "No one can forgive sins but God alone" (cf. Mk 2:7). If therefore we imitate in our own life the characteristics of the Divine Nature, we become somehow that which we visibly imitate.[2]

Jesus is not simply proposing to his followers that we should follow his example. It's actually deeper than that — much deeper. He proposes that we allow him to give us the capacity and the strength to forgive as he does, to forgive others in him.

Not surprisingly, our Lord teaches us to seek that grace, to implore it from him. In the fifth petition of the Our Father, we essentially do just that. We ask to be empowered to do what God does: to forgive that our sins might be forgiven. It is to do something divine — different in kind, in quality, in transcendence from any merely human pardoning that had been part of human experience prior to the coming of Jesus. Biblical theologian, prolific author, and speaker Scott Hahn has put it beautifully:

So, we forgive as God forgives, in imitation not only of the quantity but also the quality of His forgiveness. Like God, we forgive, not merely by forgetting, but by loving. It is the heat of God's love that melts the ice of our sin; and so it is the heat of our love that will bring about the forgiveness of those who trespass against us. We don't just remit their debts; we love our enemies into wholeness, as God has done to us. We melt their cold hearts, the ice of their sin.

Such forgiveness is an action purely divine, even when it's done by humans. Such forgiveness is possible only by humans who are being divinized.[3]

Thus in forgiving, elevated by grace to the utter newness of life in Christ, we are enabled to do a *divinized* thing as divinized beings in Christ: We are empowered to forgive as God forgives. And to do so, to forgive, places us at the apex of loving as Jesus loved.

"Father, forgive them, for they know not what they do." Our redemption, as made explicit by our Lord as he hangs from his cross, is, in its essence, about our forgiveness; about the Trinity re-creating the creature, lifting the creature to the possibility of divine life by making it the subject of divine forgiveness.

In Neal Lozano's Unbound ministry, a crucial key to inner healing is forgiveness.[4] Lozano understands this, however, not as a human capacity, but as a gift received — in the sense that we cannot give what we have not received. We need to open ourselves to receive from Jesus the capacity to forgive: "When we truly experience the power of the Gospel, which is forgiveness, our lives are changed. ... This is where forgiveness is born; this is the source, the love of Christ. What is released? The gift of love. As we receive forgiveness, we are empowered to forgive."[5]

You see this in the game of billiards or pool. Not so much forgiveness, but the process of the releasing of the power of forgiveness. In pool, if you hit the cue ball very hard, it will collide with another, and sometimes the cue ball will stop while the other ball jumps forward. The force from the first ball is transferred to the second ball. This is like forgiveness from the Lord: The impact of that forgiveness in our soul creates a certain desire or even impulse to forgive others. We experience the profound freeing aspect of being forgiven, and we want that power to radiate to others. And we want ourselves to be free from holding back forgiveness.

The foregoing considerations reveal in a sense how our Lord can *require* us to forgive. But they also point, by that same token, to the divine element in genuine Christian forgiveness. Our Lord's conditional proposition, "If you forgive ... you will be forgiven," and St. Paul's "forgive ... as the Lord has forgiven you" plainly reveal how forgiveness must be understood as a supreme expression of our Lord's *new* commandment: "Love one another *as I love you*" (Jn 15:12, emphasis added).

Much like charity, or as an expression of it, forgiveness has no value if it is coerced. This touches on the closely related and perennial question of whether love can be commanded. Our Lord appears to have done just that in John 13:34: "I give you a new commandment: love one another. As I have loved you, so you also should love one another." And to love as Christ loves is the fullest vision of what God intended in that second prong of the great dual commandment of love of God and neighbor (see Mk 12:29–31). So, can love — and within love, forgiveness — be commanded? Commenting on that seeming paradox, Pope Benedict XVI observes:

No longer is it a question, then, of a "commandment" imposed from without and calling for the impossible, but rather of a freely-bestowed experience of love from within, a love which by its very nature must then be shared with others. Love grows through love. Love is "divine" because it comes from God and unites us to God; through this unifying process it makes us a "we" which transcends our divisions and makes us one, until in the end God is "all in all" (1 Cor 15:28).[6]

The new commandment of love does not coerce our freedom; it perfects our freedom. Ever-growing intimacy with God becomes the furnace in which love, especially expressed in genuine agape-love of our neighbor, is enkindled. Jesus can command us to love as he loved because he intended to give us — from within, from our intimate interior relationship with him, through grace — the possibility of loving as he loved. Grace brings forgiveness to perfection to the extent that forgiveness is an expression of that very agape-love of neighbor.

> *Jesus can command us to love as he loved because he intended to give us — from within, from our intimate interior relationship with him, through grace — the possibility of loving as he loved.*

No doubt, there is a merely human capacity to forgive, as we have seen. Yet this pales in comparison to the superhuman reality of forgiveness in Christ. Genuine Christian forgiveness, a supreme exercise of agape-love, is always a fruit of the action of the Holy Spirit (cf., 1 Jn 4:12–13). This forgiveness, in every real-life instance of it, is a living icon of the self-revelation of the Triune God. God's deepest self-revelation through the Son is the Father's redemptive, forgiving love, laid open in the pierced heart of his Son on Calvary.

The core of God's self-revelation to the human person is: "I love you and forgive you, and in forgiving you, I reconstitute you as my beloved child and I call you to eternal communion with me." To forgive, then, to image the Father's love, to be fully caught up in the experience of transmitting this unconditional love of the Father to another human being, lies at the pinnacle of what it means to be a Christian disciple. To forgive another human being is a supreme human experience — a transformative, divinizing experience that brings us to the zenith of what it means to be human.

For Reflection and Prayer

1. Jesus expects his disciples to forgive, and he empowers us to forgive. Think about a time when you forgave someone. Did you ask for God's help as you offered forgiveness, or did you rely primarily on your own willpower? How might asking for God's grace change the way you offer forgiveness in the future, or how has doing so helped you in the past?

2. Scott Hahn wrote that when we forgive, we do a "divinized thing." Have you ever thought that you could do a "divinized thing"? How do you receive that reality? Consider bringing this possibility to prayer. What do you want to tell the Lord?

Chapter 5

The Key You've Been Looking For

Forgiveness as a Pathway to Inner Healing

So if the Son sets you free, you really will be free.

— John 8:36 (NASB)

St. Thomas Aquinas was a careful observer of human nature. He noted that sorrow and then anger are spontaneous responses to people who harm us.[1] And while we typically react to sorrow and anger negatively — because none of us enjoys being sad or angry — he observed nonetheless that these emotional responses are, at least initially, quite reasonable. A harm to our person, whether physical, psychological, or spiritual, causes sorrow, the emotion we feel when faced with the fact that we have been denied a desired good. For its part, anger arises, inclining us to seek justice or restitution in face of the good that was denied to us.

Yet these emotional responses can be treacherous. When they remain unresolved or undealt with, they can fester. Sadness and anger, over time, can give rise to resentment, loathing, contempt, rage, hatred — and unforgiveness.

In this chapter, we want to explore two closely related themes. First, we need to examine how forgiveness can lead us to an awareness of emotional wounds, opening a pathway to freedom and deeper healing in our lives.

Second, we want to reflect on the reality that, precisely because of those underlying emotional wounds, forgiveness is less of a one-time act of our will and much more a process. This process can in some cases take a long time, requiring renewed and sustained effort. Having reflected on this dynamic, we'll be all set to jump into the actual steps involved in forgiveness in chapter 6, following a spiritual road map to obtain the grace of forgiveness.

Untended Wounds Eventually Fester

Underlying our unforgiveness are emotional wounds — some small and transitory, some deep and life-changing. Any eventual healing of these wounds requires us, first of all, to acknowledge them. And guess what: That's often a difficult thing to do! In fact, part of our deep resistance to forgiveness, more unwittingly than not, resides in our unwillingness to deal with the wounds that gave rise to the unforgiveness in the first place.

Resentment is a quick fix for the pain of underlying emotional wounds that go untended. It can become a permanent fixture of our inner world if we let it. Unforgiveness is the tribute we pay to our emotional wounds. The problem with paying such tribute, and opting to self-medicate with resentment, bitterness, and antipathy toward the offender, is that we are left with festering wounds. We fail to deal with them. And this is what keeps us in emotional and spiritual chains.

Consequently, we cannot emphasize enough the relationship between forgiveness and freedom: the freedom experienced in the act of forgiving. As we have examined in the preceding chapters, forgiveness is a mutual unchaining, for both the forgiver and the forgiven. The remarkable thing about graced forgiveness is how it opens up a pathway to healing in other areas of our life. How is it then that unforgiveness acts as a roadblock to healing?

> *Unforgiveness is the tribute we pay to our emotional wounds. The problem with paying such tribute, and opting to self-medicate with resentment, bitterness, and antipathy toward the offender, is that we are left with festering wounds.*

Sandy's Story

After thirty years of marriage with Alan, Sandy discovered emails revealing that Alan had been involved for the past four years in a steamy affair with his secretary. She was crushed by what she read in some of his correspondences with his secretary, many of them written late at night, presumably after Sandy had gone to bed: "I can't live without you ..."; "You complete me ..." Sandy also came to discover the depths of Alan's porn addiction — something she had never wanted to completely acknowledge. When Sandy finally confronted him with the emails, Alan did not deny the affair, nor apologize, nor seek her forgiveness. He had "moved on," he said, with no explanation. He was just "in a different place" than he was in their earlier years of marriage.

Still, Sandy fought desperately to save their marriage:

> I forgave Alan the day I called him to come back home in order to confront him with the truth. I wanted to believe whole heartedly that our marriage commitment was as important and as sacred to him as it was to me. I believed that our marriage could withstand this blow and that we could be stronger for it. I was all-in on my forgiveness. Not that I thought this was going to be easy, but I thought we could work through it together. I couldn't imagine life without Alan. I was willing to forgive at any cost.

Months later, Sandy came to the realization that her initial act of forgiveness might have been more of an initial emotional impulse. The real, deeper work of forgiving Alan — for her own spiritual, emotional, and psychological health — was only beginning:

> It's funny, because I remember telling him the day I confronted him with the emails, that I forgave him. I truly meant it. I basically thought that he screwed up, and I made excuses in my mind for why he did what he

did. The praying for forgiveness came later, maybe after I stopped begging God to repair our marriage. For me, I forgave immediately, but the anger and sadness would almost hide the forgiveness and drive me to self-medicate in different ways. I realized that I had to keep working on forgiveness — for the sake of my own soul, not his.

Most of my friends and family thought I was crazy to even consider forgiving Alan (who has never asked me to forgive him), but I knew and still know, that I have to forgive him in order to have peace in my own soul and for God to be pleased with me. I want to hear those words one day: "Well done, my good and faithful servant."

In the first couple of years after their separation, Sandy described having to reengage in her forgiveness of Alan — like a daily discipline that she had to lean into in order to live in a newfound freedom:

There were days when the struggle to forgive consumed me so much that I laid awake at night thinking about my hurt, and how difficult it is to forgive the father of my sons who treated me like I was disposable and not worthwhile. Forgiving Alan is like having a disability. It's something I live with every day. I'm never without it. I have to forgive him so that I don't live in anger and bitterness. I don't want the hurt to make me a miserable woman.

The Obstacle in Our Way to Freedom

Sandy discovered that bitterness and anger, if left untended, would surely keep her from the freedom she desired. You see, unforgiveness acts as a roadblock, an obstacle, or spiritual and psychological blockage. Just as an intestinal blockage causes all types of pain, a spiritual blockage from unforgiveness produces a plethora of symptoms. Think about those symptoms that might indicate that you're holding a grudge, that you're angry, or unforgiving. For example, you keep replaying a scene of conflict in your head. You're not sleeping well. You're sad, irritable, sullen. You're stressed. You might even be sick. You're snapping at the kids. You're short with your spouse. You're having angry outbursts that you immediately know are out of proportion to the situation at hand. In other words, you notice steam escaping here and there. Other emotions are piling up. You find yourself less productive. Your energy level is way down. You're overeating. Perhaps your daily consumption of alcohol is on the uptick, or you notice yourself struggling with more temptations against chastity.

> *Unforgiveness is a psychic blockage as well as a spiritual blockage. That is to say, it is an obstacle to grace.*

These symptoms can indicate that there's a blockage. Unforgiveness is a psychic blockage as well as a spiritual blockage; that is to say, it is an obstacle to grace. St. Thomas says that God pours grace into the soul like sunlight into a room.[2] Obstacles to grace act like obstacles to light. No wonder, when we're in a place of unforgiveness, we might describe ourselves (or others would describe us!) as dark, dreary, sullen, gloomy, or having a cloud hanging over us. Aquinas's point is that this is precisely how sin acts as an obstacle to grace. While not all unforgiveness is deliberate and therefore sinful, it nonetheless acts to block grace.

Like Sunlight into a Room

It's not uncommon that, in forgiving, we come to find that other things are happening in us, new things, unexpected things — psychologically and spiritually — that often contribute to uncovering and healing inner wounds.

When I (Father Tom) was able to forgive one of my colleagues after a very painful blowup we had some years ago, I was surprised to discover, in the days and weeks that followed, a number of unexpected blessings. Central to this was what I learned about myself. (No surprise that in forgiving someone we can learn a lot about ourselves!) The tense moments we shared revealed that this individual had felt — *for years* — extremely put down by my attitude toward him. He had found himself all too often on the receiving end of my dismissiveness, lack of appreciation, and, sadly but honestly, my contempt. It did not help that we were so different, cut from extremely different cloth in just about every respect. It just took one tense exchange to suddenly be confronted with how deeply and how mutually we did not like each other.

Simultaneous with my asking for his forgiveness, and with my intentional act of forgiving him, came an acute awareness of how deeply I had hurt him. My asking for forgiveness, and my forgiving him, left me very vulnerable. In the course of our tense exchange, as several years of his pent-up resentment exploded in my face, I suffered what authors Doug Stone, Bruce Patton, and Sheila Heen call an "identity quake."[3] I was evidently *not* the all-around caring, compassionate person I thought I was. When I was able to forgive him for his contribution to our problematic relationship, I was also aware of being more able to serenely integrate the unhappy truth about myself. Asking his forgiveness, and forgiving him for his outburst, put me not only in a place of repentance, but also in a place of honest self-knowledge.

When we forgive, we should not be surprised that we receive

this kind of influx of the gift of knowledge. This knowledge, a gift of the Holy Spirit, transcends the human intellect's capacity. Rather, it comes to us as an infusion — a sudden insight — in regard to others, and sometimes to ourselves: to aid us in grasping the true measure of created reality, and persons, and the limitations of creatures and events. This insight helps us to achieve a deeper grasp of our real situation, of our footing in reality, and of the horizon on which we live.

The act of forgiving, in addition to bringing healthy self-knowledge, can usher in any number of other good things: empathy, gentleness, compassion, insight into the human heart.

But perhaps one of the most surprising things is the way an act of forgiveness can usher in unexpected healing in other areas of our life. And that's because an act of forgiveness has the spiritual effect of opening us up to a sudden intake of grace. The blockage is removed. Like walking into a dark room and drawing open the curtains on a sunny morning, forgiveness ushers grace into the soul. And grace has the effect of illuminating the soul.

How the Trinity Heals Us

Especially where unforgiveness lingers in us in the form of unresolved anger or hatred, resentment and antipathy, we risk living as wounded wounders. And no one wants that. The act of forgiveness, as it reveals our underlying emotional wounds, is normally a crucial step toward ongoing healing of those wounds. So how can God bring that healing about?

In God's way of healing us, healing is typically not without struggle. In fact, it should not surprise us that he very intentionally allows us to struggle. This is why healing is normally a process, especially the graced healing of emotional wounds.

The book of Joshua ends with the people of Israel, having

crossed into the promised land, facing a fundamental choice: Will they remain faithful to the Lord and to their covenant with him? Joshua admonishes them: "If it is displeasing to you to serve the LORD, choose today whom you will serve, the gods your ancestors served beyond the River or the gods of the Amorites in whose country you are dwelling. As for me and my household, we will serve the LORD" (Jos 24:15).

Unswerving, the people respond:

> Far be it from us to forsake the LORD to serve other gods. For it was the LORD, our God, who brought us and our ancestors up out of the land of Egypt, out of the house of slavery. He performed those great signs before our very eyes and protected us along our entire journey and among all the peoples through whom we passed. At our approach the LORD drove out all the peoples, including the Amorites who dwelt in the land. Therefore, we also will serve the LORD, for he is our God. (24:16–18)

This is a tremendous moment for the Chosen People. Joshua has led them into the promised land. The God who initiated their process of salvation, liberating them under Moses and Aaron from their forsaken state of slavery in Egypt, has now brought the promise to fruition. The process of gradual liberation has been accomplished. We might say that in some sense the Chosen People have experienced a national healing.

But what a hellish road to get there! The terrifying experience of flight from the Egyptians, followed by the endurance test that would be forty years of uncertainty and peril wandering in a desert, not knowing if from one day to the next there would even be water to drink. Heat, exhaustion, distrust of their leaders, anger at Moses, seemingly aimless wandering, quarrels, serpents, hunger and thirst, danger on all sides with no end in sight — and so much of this the fruit and consequence of their own frailty and infidelity to God.

Yet part of the healing revealed in this final passage from Joshua is a kind of healing of memory: "Far be it from us to abandon the LORD … for in truth … as we look back, we now see that his hand was always at work, even in the midst of our painful circumstances. In spite of our infidelity to him, he remained faithful to us. He performed all those great signs before our very eyes and protected us along our entire journey and among all the peoples through whom we passed."

God could have led his people straight away into the promised land; it could have all happened relatively quickly. Sometimes even today our Lord will bring about miraculous healings, even of emotional wounds. But just as with the Chosen People, that's not typically the course he chooses for us. Rather, the way God heals us — we might say the ordinary way — almost always evolves over time and includes an element of struggle, sometimes even mighty struggle, often precipitated by our own bad choices or the bad choices of others.

As we will see, this is why we should not be surprised that forgiveness, although it requires a very deliberate and intentional choice on our part, is not simply a one-time kind of thing. We will still find ourselves struggling with negative emotions. We will find it necessary to renew our act of forgiveness from time to time. And of course, it might take us a very long time to get to that place where we are actually ready to forgive.

It's natural for us to think of inner healing — emotional, psychological, spiritual — in terms of physical healing. With most physical healing, if you pull a muscle, or cut yourself, or twist an ankle, eventually you get back to normal. There might be a scar, but basically healing in the physical sense, in most of our mundane experiences of illness and injury, means getting back to baseline — where we were pre-injury.

If applied to the realm of emotional, psychological, and spiritual healing, the analogy to physical healing can be somewhat helpful, but it has its limits. Inner healing is different in many ways. And spiritual healing especially.

Paradoxically, many times our Lord's goal in bringing about spiritual healing is precisely not to make the inner wound go away, getting us back to our pre-injury interior baseline. This is why it should not come as a surprise, ultimately, that our interior woundedness — the hurt and the emotions attached to unforgiveness, such as anger and resentment — tend to remain. If we find ourselves struggling with those emotions, even a long time after having forgiven and prayed for healing, we shouldn't be surprised. God's healing is not necessarily about making wounds go completely away. It's much more about leading us to himself through our woundedness.

God's way of healing emotional wounds, in fact, seems to involve good days and bad, ups and downs, tough days dealing with dark clouds, painful memories, strong emotions. And all this takes time — sometimes lots of time.

God's healing is not necessarily about making wounds go completely away. It's much more about leading us to himself through our woundedness.

Ultimately, spiritual healing is nothing less than our union with God. And God does not necessarily need our wounds to go away entirely in order to bring that about. Is this not part of the Good News revealed to us in the resurrection appearances of

Jesus? He appears to the disciples — even in his glorious body — with the wounds of the crucifixion still visible!

Returning to Sandy's story, we recognize that over time she had to integrate forgiveness of Alan into her daily life. But she also sees, in retrospect, how God was working powerfully through this experience to draw her closer to himself:

> I've had to work every day over the past five years to forgive him. I think that gradually the forgiveness is getting easier to make part of my life-meaning. I'm not as anxious and sad as I was, and when I get sad or anxious, it's not as dark as it once was.

She explained how the whole long ordeal, most importantly, has brought about a transformation in her spiritual life:

> I had always wanted to live a life that is truly God-centered. That is the biggest difference in my life now. I didn't realize my life was not God-centered until it finally became God-centered. And that has to be credited in large part to the separated and divorced group I joined.
>
> These women had been divorced for a few more years than I had been. Their stories were very similar, though. But seeing their peace and ability to forgive after long term marriages (basically, like me they had devoted their lives to one man, one marriage) was a benchmark for me. I wanted to have the joy and peace in my heart that they exuded.
>
> They encouraged me to go to a weekend retreat for divorced men and women. This weekend, along with several other retreats I've attended, helped build the peace and quiet in my heart that I yearned for.

As Sandy discovered, engaging in the ongoing process of forgiving over time became like a key to open pathways of healing in her own life, and to discover a deepened relationship with God. As we have been at pains to emphasize, forgiveness is seldom a one-and-done kind of thing. It takes time. God's healing of our emotional wounds takes time — and forgiving can be a catalyst for that healing.

To forgive someone who has offended us is a form of healing. And when we forgive in the power of Jesus, his grace can usher in and release profound healing in our lives. We're now in a good position to explore in detail, in the following chapter, the actual process of forgiveness, the road map to forgiveness, we might say, and to open our lives to its healing power.

For Reflection and Prayer

1. This chapter discusses the fallout from harboring unforgiveness. Are you typically aware when you are unforgiving, perhaps holding a grudge? What behaviors — or changes in your behavior — indicate this?

2. Take some time, serenely and honestly, in the presence of our Lord, simply to become aware of any areas of unforgiveness in your life. It could be for something minor or something major, involving a recent offense or a past offense. Become aware of what you are feeling. Name the feelings. (This exercise will be very helpful in preparation for what you will learn in chapter 6.)

Part Two

Forgiveness: The Process and the Possibilities

Chapter 6
So How Do We Do It?

Forgiveness In a Four-Step Process

Joseph replied to them: "Do not fear. ... Even though you
meant harm to me, God meant it for good, to achieve
this present end, the survival of many people. So now, do
not fear. I will provide for you and for your children."

— *Genesis 50:19–21*

We hope the preceding chapters have helped you understand the deeper dynamics and challenges of forgiveness.
We also hope you understand that God, by his grace, can elevate
and empower forgiveness to unleash healing in your life. You

might be saying to yourself, "I never knew forgiveness was so complicated!" But *forgiveness* isn't complicated. *We* are!

We also hope the preceding chapters have disabused you of the notion that forgiveness means forgive, forget, and move on. That may be true for the minor irritations in life. But for the bigger hurts, forgiveness is going to be a process. In this chapter, we want to explain that process. The approach we'll present is based on decades of research about forgiveness by both secular and Christian psychologists.

The best research comes from Catholic psychologist and psychology professor at the University of Wisconsin–Madison, Dr. Robert Enright, and Christian psychologist and psychology professor emeritus at Virginia Commonwealth University, Dr. Everette Worthington Jr. These two academics were pioneers in the scientific study of forgiveness and were key players in kicking off this new field of study that has exploded over the last thirty years. Dr. Enright was the first to bring forgiveness into the laboratory, and he was later followed by Dr. Worthington, as they both tried to empirically understand what is happening as we forgive. They and their colleagues, as well as hundreds of researchers following their lead, have continued to seek understanding of forgiveness; and they have also taken what they've learned and applied it in different settings — for example, in elementary schools in Northern Ireland in order to help Protestant and Catholic children learn how to forgive. And the process works. These academics have found evidenced-based approaches to forgiveness that not only make sense spiritually and theologically, but also scientifically.[1]

There are many different paths to forgiveness. One size does not fit all. The research offers many guidelines that are consistent with our experience. Drs. Worthington and Enright and their colleagues have outlined a series of steps that enable us to understand the journey of forgiveness and to enter the process with clarity and greater ease. In this chapter, we will explain a four-step process of forgiveness that closely follows Enright's method while incorporating the wisdom of Worthington's method and several other paths of forgiveness.[2] The beauty of following these steps is that we can return to them again and again. In other words, we don't need to reinvent the forgiveness wheel every time someone hurts us. We can simply reenter the process, guided by these steps that we have based on theirs.

The four steps of forgiveness are: uncovering, deciding, proclaiming, and deepening. But before we walk through these steps, we need to unpack the idea that forgiveness is a process — not simply one discrete action in time — and that it requires a positive attitude.

Forgiveness Is a Process

Consider what forgiving is *un*like — ordering takeout from a restaurant, for example. Ordering takeout is easy: We submit an order, pay for it, and walk away with our food. If only forgiveness were that easy! In reality, and in most cases, forgiveness takes place as a process. And when it comes to forgiving offenses that have left the deepest wounds? Forgiveness is more like a marathon, no matter how much we would prefer it to be a sprint. To put it another way, forgiveness is often more like a journey than a destination.

Many Catholics have the mistaken idea that they can say the magic words, "I forgive you," and everything will be all better. Psychologists call this "magical thinking" because forgiveness almost always requires patience, time, consistent effort, endurance, and fortitude. We all have to work at forgiveness, even those rare people who seem to forgive with little effort. For all of us, it can often seem to be sheer drudgery. With God's grace, however, it can actually become a labor of love. If you follow the process, and progress along the steps we will describe, you can be sure that over time the frustration, irritation, anger, and hatred can begin to melt. As a frozen lake slowly thaws in the spring, so the forgiveness process slowly shifts our emotional reactions, deepens our healing, and brings us satisfaction and relief.

The Right Attitude

Success in the process of forgiving presupposes a positive attitude about forgiveness. We won't last in this effort if we're not convinced that forgiveness is a good thing. We may not be good at it. We may struggle with it. We may even dislike it. But we have to know, in some deep part of our heart and mind, that forgiveness is a good thing.

> *As a frozen lake slowly thaws in the spring, so the forgiveness process slowly shifts our emotional reactions, deepens our healing, and brings us satisfaction and relief.*

What we're talking about here is the conviction that abundant life includes abundant forgiveness: I will only flourish as a human being if I put into practice, again and again, the process of forgiveness. That positive attitude can become in us a ready disposition, a default willingness, to engage in the process as many times as necessary whenever we are confronted with hurts, offenses, or abuse from others. We might think of this positive attitude as an umbrella that allows us to face inclement weather. As long as we're under the umbrella, we're fine with walking in the rain.

A consistent positive attitude will grow and accrue over time as we experience, over and over, the freedom of forgiveness. The bottom line is, we have to *want* to forgive. So if we want to forgive, even though we may struggle mightily, we're in a good place to move forward. If you're ready now, and you're under the umbrella, let's enter the rain!

Step 1: Uncovering

The first step to forgiveness is uncovering. This step invites us to examine our heart, examine the situation and the persons involved, and then identify where we lack forgiveness. Uncovering involves overcoming certain obstacles that can prevent us from seeing our situation honestly. First and foremost, we have to unmask any false or knee-jerk forgiveness we might have already given to the person or persons in question.

We recommend that you begin this step by asking, "Where was I offended?" or "What needs to be forgiven?" To that end, this step invites us to specifically identify those moments when an experience was hurtful, or someone's actions offended us, or someone treated us unjustly. Again, we suspend the sense that "I've already forgiven them." Usually that sentiment simply means we want to believe we've forgiven because then we don't have to do the hard work of forgiving. In those knee-jerk cases, we have to be honest and be open to accept that we might *not* have fully forgiven. More times than not, there is more to forgive. Once we've uncovered the hurtful situations using the steps that follow, we will need to decide what we want to do, and then act on that decision.

We'll examine these steps by following the case of Mike. I (Dr. Lock) have based Mike's story on that of many clients I've worked with over the years. The movements of Mike's heart, and the gradual impact of working through the steps of forgiveness, capture the experience of multiple clients I've accompanied on the path of forgiveness using the four-step process.

Mike had been seemingly happily married for thirteen years, though the marriage, like most, had its challenges. Nevertheless, feeling restless and struggling with the demands of family life and a growing career, he had fallen in love with a colleague at the office. He was going out to lunch with her on a regular basis and was strongly tempted to take things a lot further than lunch. He was considering throwing in the towel and engaging in a full-blown affair. Feeling torn apart inside, he recognized that he needed help and made an appointment with me.

Together, as we reviewed the twists and turns of his life, Mike realized that his relationship with his older brother, Sam, left him with serious wounds from childhood. You might be wondering how something from so long ago could be related to his current crisis, but from my clinical perspective, and based on years of experience, they were clearly connected. Eventually, Mike agreed. Allow me to explain.

As we spoke over numerous sessions, it became clear that Sam was actually often kind to Mike — the negative treatment was not the norm. On three occasions, however, Sam harassed Mike sexually through inappropriate touching, episodes that Mike now recognizes as sexual abuse. He teared up as he shared, in detail, what he had experienced. He also remembered that one day, after the third time that Sam abused him, Mike made a vow that he would *never* forgive his brother for what he had done. Interestingly, soon after that vow, his brother went to college and never spent much time at home again. Somehow, Mike believed that his vow protected him against future attacks from Sam. He spent a few months working through his feelings associated with these traumas, and as the intensity of the emotions began to subside, Mike knew what he had to do next. He needed to forgive and to renounce his vow.

Mike had completed the first step, that of uncovering. Now he was ready to look at the next step. We'll come back to his story later in step 2.

Step 2: Deciding

The second step is deciding. We have to *decide* if we want to forgive. When you are driving and come to a fork in the road, you have to decide to take a left or a right. With forgiveness, you have to decide if you are going to forgive or decide if you are *not* going to forgive. When I (Dr. Lock) describe this step to clients, some stare at me with a perplexed look. The notion that forgiveness is a choice is foreign to many people. And many Christians feel like they are trapped in a mindset that is obligating them to forgive, like they have no choice in the matter. Yet with each offense we endure, we do have a choice to forgive or a choice to *not* forgive. I emphasize to my clients that it's up to them to decide, saying, "Ask yourself, with each of these offenses: 'Do I want to forgive?'"

To forgive or not to forgive? That is, indeed, the question.

To forgive or not to forgive? That is, indeed, the question. Sometimes, from deep within, you will sense yourself saying, "Yes, I want to forgive this." Other times you'll sense yourself saying, "No way! There's no way I want to forgive this!" This step requires brutal honesty. Radical honesty. Radical acceptance of the movements far down within us.

This step takes us deep into our humanity, and there we see the complexities of the human heart. Yet when we practice radical honesty, we sometimes find ourselves in a dilemma with forgiveness: Despite the fact that we know forgiveness is a good thing, despite the fact that we have a general attitude of forgiveness, despite the fact that we pray, "Forgive us our trespasses *as we forgive* those who trespass against us" (see Mt 6:12, emphasis added), sometimes our heart is not ready. "More tortuous than anything is the human heart, beyond remedy; who can understand it?" (Jer 17:9). But that's where our heart is — we're just not ready to forgive. And that's completely OK.

In order to make this as clear as possible, here's what you can do. Take a piece of paper and divide it into three columns. The first column is for the things that you are ready to forgive, the second column is for the things that you are not ready to forgive, and the third column is for the things that you are not sure you are ready to forgive. Then look plainly at your situation, consider the different incidents where forgiveness might be called for, and put each into the appropriate column.

Categories 2 and 3 — not ready to forgive and not sure you are ready to forgive — must be approached differently from category 1. With categories 2 and 3, you can simply bring them to the Lord and say, "Lord, I have these things. I'm not ready — or I don't know if I'm ready — so please work in my heart. I'm turning this over to you and I ask that you help me out. Amen." Another psychologist recommended this prayer, "Lord, *you* forgive him — I don't want to!"

The important point here is that we don't hold onto it. We don't stay stuck in a hole. We don't harbor unforgiveness. We bring it somewhere. We do something with it. Whatever we say or however we articulate it, we want to give it to Jesus. We leave it at the Lord's feet and allow him to move in our heart. At the same time, we can review step 1 — uncovering — again. This creates time for the Lord's grace to seep into our hearts, and time for our heart to shift items toward category 1.

Back to Mike. He knew what he had to do. He shared with me that throughout his life he had been faithful to his vow to never forgive his brother. But he was unsettled about this now and wasn't sure why. I told him that many people would say that the proper Catholic response would be to immediately forgive Sam and move on. But, I insisted, it's not as simple as that, especially when talking about something like abuse from his older brother. This so-called "proper" response is really a denial of our humanity. Because the process of forgiveness requires time and reflection, we have to work through the process in order to move on. "You have uncovered several traumatic incidents," I told Mike. "You've taken the first step in the forgiveness process, but the second step is deciding. You have a choice. Mike, do you *want* to forgive Sam?"

Mike had been sitting opposite me, slumped in his chair. He snapped his head down and to the right. He shrank further into the chair with a disturbed expression on his face. There were some moments of silence. He raised his gaze, but his angst prevented him from lifting his head high enough to look me in the eye. "No," he said softly, "I want to beat the crap out of him." After another long pause, he went on to talk about the humiliation that he still felt and the rage that he was tapping into as he considered making a decision to forgive Sam. He was embarrassed because he knew that was the "wrong" Catholic answer. "A Catholic should always forgive," he said, "and forgive quickly ..."

It was a tense moment. But in reality, Mike was fully engaged with step two. He was wrestling with deciding. He told me he had to think and pray about it, but thanked me for being with him through his struggles. He was glad he wasn't walking this path alone. I was glad, too. It's tough to navigate these waters all alone.

I knew we wouldn't meet again for six weeks because Mike had summer vacation ahead as well as some travel for business. Eventually he returned for another session and said, quite honestly, that he had felt tremendous pain after our last meeting.

Every time he thought about his brother or the therapy, he felt horrible. But what he shared next was unexpected and extraordinary. His wife had signed him up to help with his parish's Bible camp. This, he said, was what changed his life.

Like many a parish Bible camp, this was a somewhat disorganized smorgasbord of Jesus music, crafts, skits, kids yelling, and classic outdoor games like tag. Some of the teenage assistants roped Mike and a couple of the other parents into helping perform a skit about Jacob's son, Joseph, who was sold into slavery by his brothers. (If you don't know the story, see Genesis 45.)

As it turns out, the youth leaders cast Mike in the role of Joseph who, in that Bible story, forgives his brothers for having sold him into slavery. When it came to that moment in the production, Mike was overwhelmed with emotion. He laughed as he told me, "I couldn't say the words of my script. Tears were streaming down my face as I squeaked out the lines where Joseph forgives his brothers. I was an absolute mess. And get this: At the end of the scene, the little kids in the audience applauded like I have never heard before. Afterward, people were telling me that I was such a great actor. They thought I was conjuring up those tears. Little did they know, they weren't tears for the brothers of Joseph. They were tears for my own brother."

Mike was ready to forgive. He wanted to forgive. He decided to repent of his vow and give his brother a gift: the gift of forgiveness.

Step 3: Proclaiming

The third step is proclaiming. What are we proclaiming? That we have made the decision and that we forgive that person who offended us with our whole heart (or as much of our heart as we can). To whom are we making this proclamation? To ourselves and to the Lord. But what about the person we're forgiving? In chapter 9 we'll talk about telling the offender that you forgive them, but first, at this point, you must be able to say — to yourself and to the Lord — that you forgive the offender. For now, let's stay focused on what's going on in your mind and heart as the person who is choosing to forgive.

Some people call this step "the act of forgiving" because it is here that we muster the courage to say the words, "I forgive you." This act is not really an action in the manner that, say, chopping firewood or pouring a cup of coffee are actions. The act of forgiveness is more an act of the will. In this step, we say it. We own it. We mean it — even if we might not yet *feel* it. If the process of forgiveness is like jumping off a diving board: step 1 (uncovering) is climbing up the ladder to the diving board; step 2 (deciding) is like walking to the edge of the diving board; step 3 (proclaiming) is jumping off the diving board. We can say it out loud or in our heart, but either way, we say it. We say it to ourselves, and we say it to God.

There are three parts to proclaiming this act of forgiveness: (1) saying, "I forgive ..."; (2) saying the person's name; and (3) saying exactly what you are forgiving the person for. The act of forgiveness could sound like this: "I forgive Jack for ignoring me at that party," or "Lord, I forgive my husband for scraping the paint off the car when he opened the door and hit the brick wall," or "I forgive Lucia for lying about doing her homework."

You might be surprised to see that such a momentous act can be captured in such a brief formula. Needless to say, you could make an act of forgiveness simply by speaking the appropriate words out loud or in your heart. In our experience, however, people get the maximum benefit from this step by *proclaiming to God*, in the context of a prayer, that they are forgiving the person who offended them.

A simple forgiveness prayer might sound like this: "Lord, I come before you today and ask for your help as I make this act of forgiveness. Lord, I forgive my dad for divorcing my mom when I was in grammar school, and for not visiting me throughout childhood, and for not even having a relationship with me until I was in college."

One of the most famous Catholic mental health pioneers is the psychiatrist Dr. Conrad Baars. Dr. Baars integrated the teachings of the Church, particularly those of St. Thomas Aquinas, with sound psychological principles to approach psychotherapy. A survivor of a Nazi concentration camp, he had profound insights into the pain in the human heart, and the potential for healing available through a faith-filled, integrated approach to counseling. Dr. Baars recommended this prayer for forgiveness:

> My Jesus, I visualize this person who has wronged me; I visualize him (or her) in Your merciful presence, and I say: "I forgive you _____ in the name of Jesus Christ. I also ask Jesus to forgive you for the wrong you have done to me. I give thanks to God because you are now forgiven. Amen."[3]

You can use Dr. Baars's prayer, or our prayer above, or you can find various prayers online that express forgiveness. And you most certainly can write your own.

Because forgiveness is not a casual act, much more can go into it than the prayer itself, as we have seen so far. We recommend that you make a thoughtful plan for carrying out this step. Consider proceeding along these lines as you prepare to make your proclamation of forgiveness:

- Set aside a particular time and place when you will prayerfully and formally make your proclamation.
- Find a favorite forgiveness prayer or write a forgiveness prayer of your own.

- When the day comes, at the designated time, go to the place you have chosen — maybe a church or a chapel, maybe before Jesus during Eucharistic Adoration, perhaps in a prayer corner of your home, or in a beautiful place out in nature.
- Sit comfortably and, as you settle down, open yourself to God's presence and love.
- When you are ready, pray your prayer of forgiveness.
- Record the date and time of your proclamation in a journal or diary so that you can refer to it in the future.

Why be so formal about it? Because it's important that you are able to look back and say that on this specific day, at this specific hour, in this specific setting, you sat down in prayer and forgave the person who offended you, naming the specific offense or offenses. For example: "On February 3, 2017, at 5:00 p.m., I forgave my abuser," or "I forgave my spouse," or "I forgave my parent," — or whomever — "for these particular wrongs against me." It's kind of like date stamping a photograph. Have you ever looked at a photo and wondered, "When did I take that picture?" or "When was it that I took that trip?" or "When did I see that long lost friend?" Thanks to the date stamp, you know.

Forgiveness is not a casual act.

With forgiveness, setting a date and time provides a reference point that you can revisit when you wonder, "Did I really do that? Did I really forgive them?" If you do question whether or not you've forgiven, it will usually be because unforgiveness is welling up again. With that date stamp, you can confidently say, "Yes, I did forgive," and then you can renew your forgiveness. Psychologically, the set time and place fix the event in history — you can always remember the day you jumped off the diving board.

Optimizing Step 3

Before the day arrives and you set out for that special place, you might want to consider a few additional points regarding what you are about to do. First, you want to be ready to forgive. Think about this as a recap of step 2, deciding. This act of forgiveness is something you've mulled over for a long time. Drawing from the discernment advice of St. Ignatius of Loyola, we want to emphasize that when you have decided, in peace, to forgive, you should go forward with that decision even if you are *not* in peace on the day of forgiveness.[4]

It's important to acknowledge — and not be surprised by — the fact that you may not feel very forgiving when the day to proclaim forgiveness rolls around. Remember, forgiveness is a decision that occurs despite your feelings. Even after the proclamation, you may still have negative feelings. This is normal. It doesn't mean anything except that your feelings are not yet in sync with your will. Following these steps usually brings a shift in those emotions, but at this point in the process you may not experience a profound affective shift.

If you have decided to forgive but feel stuck at the proclamation point, here are some techniques to help you reconsider your thoughts about the offender if those thoughts are inhibiting your decision to forgive.

The first is a cognitive technique that can help shift your point of view so that you can look at the offender and the offense differently. For example, attempting to understand the person who hurt you and *why* they hurt you can help. Your intent here is not to provide them with an excuse or to let them off the hook or to minimize the hurt they caused. Rather, doing this exercise can help you have a sense, however small, about how someone could hurt another human being in the way they have hurt you. Take the time to consider a little bit about the offender's strengths and gifts and talents, as well as their flaws and blind spots and brokenness and sin.

What was going on in the mind and heart of the offender at the time of the offense, for example? What was going on in the time leading up to the offense? What about the offender's past and the events in their childhood and teenage years might have set them up to commit the offense? What experiences in their life may have formed them to do such a thing? In some instances, you might realize that the offender's intention was good but poorly expressed. In other instances, you might see that the offender's distorted past led him to commit wicked deeds. Our point is that, as people consider the different perspectives, they sometimes come to see the offender less as a monster and more as a wounded person — the phrase "hurt people hurt people" comes to mind. Taking this shift in perspective is not always easy. In cases of serious harm, we would expect that a counselor or priest will help you navigate these questions so that you can prudently review your situation.

The emotion-focused technique involves revisiting the situation in your mind and allowing yourself to experience the feelings that rise up. Talking with a trusted friend or family member may help you in this process, as might recording your thoughts in a journal. This kind of "expressive" writing, in particular, can help remove the emotional haze that frequently occurs when we revisit traumatic events and consider those who have harmed us.[5] Coming at this from another vantage point, you can try to understand and feel what the offender was feeling. This provides yet another perspective for us as we try to wrap our head around the experience that hurt us.

Don't be surprised if these exercises lead you to feel an element of compassion, pity, or mercy toward the offender. Let the feelings come, but don't force yourself to feel anything in particular. Simply allow the natural healing to emerge. Expect to experience some grace from the Lord as you grapple with these approaches. Also, you can use these same techniques as you work through steps 2 and 4 — or really, whenever they might help move you forward — and not only as you get set to proclaim forgiveness in step 3.

Finally, we want to reinforce the need to be specific, to be focused. Avoid forgiving a "situation" or forgiving a group of people — in other words, don't offer the sort of blanket forgiveness or broad statement designed to cover a multitude of offenses. Be specific. Don't do this, for example: "I forgive my wife for everything." Our Lord loves us each individually and uniquely, and in the same manner we want to offer this gift of forgiveness as fully and as specifically as possible. We give this gift to a particular person, for a particular reason. Here's how a proclamation can look when it's specific and when the harm inflicted has multiple components: "Lord, I forgive Jack [my husband], for screaming at me, calling me a loser, and walking away. I forgive him for coming back into the room and giving me that look of disgust and walking away again. I forgive him for

> *Avoid forgiving a "situation" or forgiving a group of people — in other words, don't offer the sort of blanket forgiveness or broad statement designed to cover a multitude of offenses. Be specific.*

leaving the house and not returning for twenty-four hours. I forgive him for returning and acting as if nothing happened. And I forgive him for not remembering the event when I attempted to discuss and resolve it with him a week later."

When you finish your proclamation and when you finish your prayer time before the Lord, take a moment to thank Jesus for his goodness to you. Thank him for leading you down this path of forgiveness and helping you to proclaim your forgiveness. Allow yourself to rest in that forgiveness, to soak in the experience.

I (Dr. Lock) led Mike through this third step, inviting him to use journaling as a vehicle to explore his feelings toward Sam and to understand elements of the past, things that Mike was able to remember about Sam's own childhood. Those things that left Sam wounded and that predisposed him to hurt others, including Mike. This ended up being a very fruitful exercise that helped prepare Mike for making the act of forgiveness. When he executed his plan for proclaiming, and he was finally able to say the words "I forgive Sam," he told me that the event was a bit anticlimactic. There was no Alleluia chorus. There were no earthquakes, no tears, no drama. Just a deep sense of serenity. Mike knew that he was free, even though he was aware that he would need to deepen his forgiveness over time and probably have to recommit to forgiving Sam if feelings of unforgiveness reemerged.

Step 4: Deepening

The fourth step is called "deepening." After the proclamation, we want to rest in this state of forgiveness, not simply for a moment, but for our lifetime. And so, after the proclamation, we round out the experience by allowing the forgiveness to be strengthened, to be enriched, and to deepen. Further, within the constraints of our situation, we perform acts of love for the one we have forgiven. We pray for them, for example, or we resume those acts of friendship that were a hallmark of the relationship prior to the rupture, such as initiating a phone call or meeting for lunch. Using our diving board analogy, step 3 was diving off the diving board, and step 4, deepening, occurs as we swim in the pool after having jumped off the diving board. We swim in the waters of forgiveness.

As noted in step 3, cognitive and emotive techniques can be useful in the deepening phase. Here, as we rest in forgiveness, we reflect on the situation and on the offender. We widen our point of view, and we allow ourselves to feel whatever feelings come forth, deepening our experience of forgiveness. We can begin to see, with clarity, what we may consider doing to extend love to the person who hurt us. Resting in these thoughts can be like relaxing on a raft in the swimming pool of forgiveness.

During the deepening phase, however, there may be times when feelings of unforgiveness well up. This is bound to happen, and it's normal. With regard to the very deepest hurts that we have suffered, a certain persistent feeling of anger toward the perpetrator might always accompany our forgiveness. This could be entirely appropriate, and it doesn't mean that we have failed to forgive. The ongoing assault of such strong feelings can indicate, also, that our mind and heart need time to absorb our profound act of forgiveness. We want to protect ourselves from being hurt again, and the reemergence of unforgiveness is, in some way, our body's effort to protect ourselves against the hurt.

Often, however, persistent feelings of rage and resentment need tempering. Here's the best response you can have when feelings of unforgiveness well up: Be gentle with yourself and avoid self-shaming. Don't say, "I can't believe I'm doing it again." Rather, say, "Oh, I'm human — Lord, I need your grace." Next, take a deep breath and seek to maintain your peace. Then, when you have a moment to reflect, simply turn your mind back to the individual and make the act of forgiveness again — prayerfully, of course — in that same settled spirit of prayer in which you proclaimed forgiveness in step 3. Give it all to the Lord: the person you are re-forgiving and the fact that you have experienced a reemergence of unforgiveness. You can do this over and over again as the need arises. Sincerely recommit to the decision to forgive.

Dr. Conrad Baars suggests the following prayer for this recommitment:

> Lord, it is now several days later, and I again feel some stirring of the past anger and resentment toward this person. I thank You that You have forgiven _____, and that You gave me the strength and good will to forgive him (or her). I now Bless _____ (name of wrongdoer I have forgiven) in the Name of the Lord. I see _____ as a child of God, for through my intercessory prayers God's healing love is entering into him (or her). Amen.[6]

These are the steps of forgiveness that genuinely help people to forgive. Empirical research has demonstrated their effectiveness, and we and many others have seen it ourselves through clinical practice, pastoral experience, and in the many stories we have heard from people who have put these steps into practice, as we have ourselves.

As for Mike, he spent a few months in the deepening phase and enjoyed resting in the forgiveness. From time to time, he would feel unforgiveness toward Sam well up, but he was able to navigate his way through the adverse emotions and reaffirm his forgiveness.

But what about Mike's temptation to have an affair, the original reason he had sought counseling? The abuse he had suffered at the hands of his older brother had made him overly compliant; he never disagreed with his wife, and he never complained about anything she did. Because of the abuse, he had what's known as "learned helplessness" and had lost his ability to be assertive. He had no agency, no sense of self, in close interpersonal relationships. Because Mike was passive in his relationship with his wife, he resented her and was dissatisfied with her.

Little by little, as he worked through his emotions related to the abuse, his voice at home began to grow. His wife had always longed for Mike to be more assertive, and she welcomed this new development. Early in the course of his therapy, Mike discontinued his lunches with the female colleague, and eventually his interest in her dissipated as he renewed his relationship with his wife. In working through the entire process with its many layers, Mike was able to realistically assess his situation, take the necessary steps to forgive his brother, enter the healing process in his relationship with his wife, and ultimately save his marriage.

$\sim$

Now, you don't need a therapist to guide you through the process of forgiveness. What you need is goodwill and openness to the grace our Lord wants to give you. Embrace these steps with faith in him. Let yourself be led by the impulse of agape-love and allow his power to lead you to the freedom for which you long.

Chapter 7
Going Deep

The Whole-Life Forgiveness Exercise

*Forgiveness is not weak. It takes courage to face and
overcome powerful emotions.*

— *Desmond Tutu*

Once we understand the four-step process of forgiveness, we
can apply it to our entire life. This, of course, will involve a
considerable investment of time.

When we apply what we're calling the whole-life forgiveness
exercise, we reflect on our life as far back as we can, attempting
to uncover offenses that others have committed against us. Some

people automatically reject the idea of going all the way back to the beginning, saying, "I don't want to dredge up the past unnecessarily." That's understandable — we all like to let sleeping dogs lie. But if we want to experience the fullest and deepest level of healing and freedom, we'd do well to take an honest look at our baggage to see what we can leave behind.

The whole-life forgiveness exercise follows the same four-step process outlined in the previous chapter: uncovering, deciding, proclaiming, and deepening. When we're addressing a single incident, as we discussed in chapter 6, we uncover it, we decide if we want to forgive the person who offended us, we formally proclaim our forgiveness to ourselves and to the Lord, then we rest in that state of forgiveness, allowing it to deepen. In the whole-life forgiveness exercise, we walk through those steps for the various hurts that come to mind across the span of our life up to this point. Let's see how this works, step by step.

Whole Life Forgiveness

Step 1: Uncovering

As you reflect on your life, different incidents of hurt and unforgiveness may come to mind. The time your coworker insulted you and couched it as a joke, for example. Or the time in high school when your mother unjustly punished you for messing up the kitchen while your little brother, who was the guilty party, got away without any consequences. What about the kid who bullied you in second grade? Or that time your wife returned the Christmas gift you gave her because she was mad at you. Once you start casting your mind back, you'll most likely have no trouble recalling various incidents. You might find, however, that your mind is jumping around to different phases of your life, different people, and different types of hurts. To help you handle the long timeline you'll be considering, a systematic approach will help you walk through the whole-life forgiveness process more effectively.

Here's what we suggest. Divide your life into segments so that you can record your hurts or unforgiveness in an organized fashion, according to the natural segments of your life. We offer one way to do that in this chart.

The Periods of Life

Child-hood	Teenage years	20s	30s	40s	50s	60s	70s	80s

This chart divides your life by decade, an approach that works great for some people, but not necessarily for everyone. We offer this as an example and encourage you to develop the divisions that are meaningful to you. You might base the periods on significant events, for example: from birth to preschool, preschool to fifth grade, middle school, high school, college through your early twenties, your first apartment, owning your own home up until the time your best friend died, and so on. Divide your life into whatever segments make the most sense to you, keeping in mind that the segments don't have to be of equal length. One segment could last for six months and another for twenty years. What matters most is that the segments resonate with you.

After you've broken your life into different periods, take a pad of paper or a journal, and devote one page each to every time period. Once you've done this, you're ready to start uncovering incidents that warrant forgiveness. We recommend that you begin with prayer; it could be something like this: "Holy Spirit, enlighten the eyes of my heart to see where and to whom I need to offer forgiveness in these periods of my life. Thanks for these revelations, Lord. Please continue to bring them on."

There are two approaches to uncovering these incidents: the life dump or the systematic review. We recommend that you

Take the situations where you're not ready to forgive or you're not sure you're ready to forgive, and park them with Jesus: "Lord, this is just too much for me right now. As I struggle with the memory of these experiences, help my heart to forgive."

use both, but begin with the life dump. Simply and spontaneously let hurts or offenses that warrant forgiveness come to mind from any time period of your life. As the incidents arise, flip through your journal and write them down on the page dedicated to the appropriate time period. Typically, when people begin the life dump, incidents and people from many time periods will come to mind rather quickly, sometimes faster than they can write them down. If this happens to you, don't inhibit any of your mind's ramblings. Don't censor any of it. Just write it down as fast as you can, even if the things seem really small or insignificant. Don't think about it too much, just jot a little note here, a little note there, enough to help you remember as you do your review later. When the number of these events starts to dwindle, you're ready to begin the systematic review.

To do the systematic review, you'll pick one time period of your life and write down further notes or memories regarding the situations of woundedness; hurts for which you might want to offer forgiveness. You can start this review wherever you want — in the present, or childhood, or with that one incident in college that's quietly haunted you for years. Begin wherever it makes the most sense for you.

How much time should you spend writing about and reflecting on incidents from each segment of your life? Again, you'll tailor this to your individual circumstance. Some people devote a day each to every period of their life, focusing their reflections and prayers on that segment. Some people devote their daily prayer time over a week for each segment. If you're working with a counselor or a spiritual director, you can ask them to help you know when you are "finished" with one time period and ready for the next. Being finished is hard to quantify, however. It's not like finishing a bag of M&Ms — when the bag is empty, you're finished! In the uncovering phase of the whole-life exercise, finished is more a matter of discernment, of determining when you can say "done," or maybe better, "done for now."

Once you've recorded all the incidents for each of the segments of your timeline, you're almost finished with the first step of the forgiveness process, the uncovering. Before going to the next step, take a few moments and, starting with the earliest time in your life, skim through each page of notes. As you go through your life in chronological order, some additional moments of woundedness may surface. This is normal. The brain stores memories in various ways, and this last pass through your notes allows your brain to connect the dots between events, and possibly raise additional instances of unforgiveness that were hiding in your memory. Once you've skimmed through your life, you're ready for the next step.

Step 2: Deciding

As you look at each situation by itself and recall the incident and the person involved, ask yourself, "Do I want to forgive?" Just as with the deciding step in chapter 6, you'll have three categories of response: yes, no, and maybe. Take the situations where you're not ready to forgive or you're not sure you're ready to forgive, and park them with Jesus: "Lord, this is just too much for me right now. As I struggle with the memory of these experiences, help my heart to forgive."

For the remaining events where you've been hurt but are ready to forgive, make the decision, saying to yourself that, yes, I do want to forgive this person for that. Now you'll bring those people and incidents into step 3, the formal act of forgiveness.

Step 3: Proclaiming

When you are ready to proclaim your forgiveness for all the events you have recorded and considered within the whole-life forgiveness exercise, remember the significance of what you are about to do. Renew your trust in the grace and healing our Lord wants to give you. Since you have done so much work reviewing and re-reviewing your life, we recommend that you give yourself time to really engage this step of the process. If possible, we recommend that you go to confession and Mass the day of your proclamation within the whole-life forgiveness exercise. In confession, you could take advantage of the opportunity to repent of any unforgiveness you have harbored in your heart, and to truly renounce any unforgiveness that might cling there. This will optimally dispose you to receive the many graces our Lord wants to give you.

That proclamation of forgiveness can be done in the quiet of your own home, a church, during Eucharistic Adoration, or in whatever setting you find conducive to prayer. If you are worried that it might make you cry or experience strong emotions, a solitary place might be a better option. The key thing in making this act of forgiveness is actually making the act of forgiveness. Whether you do so in a chapel, in a church, or a chapel in your heart, you will be entering into a day of profound grace.

As you prayerfully proclaim forgiveness, make sure you are as specific as possible. "Lord, I forgive [state the name of the person] for [state the behavior that was offensive or warrants forgiveness — and you should say when this offensive behavior took place]." We want you to be specific so that there are no lingering questions in your mind about the actual offenses or about your forgiveness of the persons who committed those offenses.

Record the date of your proclamation in a journal for future reference. It will look something like this: "On [this date] at [this time], I forgave [state the name of the person] for all of the behaviors that I listed above in my 'Act of Forgiveness.'" Then put down your pen and journal and take a moment to look with the eyes of your heart upon our Lord Jesus Christ who loves you and cares for you. He is proud of you. He is rejoicing with you. Take a moment to soak in the graces of this moment. Thank our heavenly Father for his providence. Thank Jesus for his assistance. Thank the Holy Spirit for his power poured out on you. Thank you, Lord!

Step 4: Deepening

When you walk away from your time with the Lord, having proclaimed forgiveness, you are now ready to enter into the phase of deepening, allowing that experience of forgiveness to resonate and take hold. As we noted earlier, as the deepening phase goes on, over days and months, inevitably you might experience feelings of unforgiveness welling up. At these times, remember that feelings are transitory. They are normal and, in light of the deepest hurts, reasonable and to be expected. Even in the midst of the adverse feelings, in these moments it is possible to renew the decision you've already made to forgive. In those moments of struggle, it can help to ask yourself once again: Do I want the best for this person who hurt me? Do I want every blessing for this person? Your "yes" to those questions renews the forgiveness you've already given.

Finally, what we described in the previous chapter applies

here especially, in the context of the whole-life forgiveness exercise and the stage of deepening: It can help to step back in order to see things from different perspectives. Doing so can increase your sense of empathy for the offender and help you to sort out negative feelings, like hate and the longing for revenge, from justifiable feelings of indignation and even anger. As you come to a clearer understanding of what may have led the offender to do what they did, you can often come to see how our Lord was able to use these unfortunate and hurtful events for the good.

~

Doing the whole-life forgiveness exercise is a big job. But your willingness to go there, to invest the time and energy, and to face potentially strong emotions is really something beautiful. Remember, though: You can't do this on your own. You need to do it in prayer. You need to open yourself to Jesus, allowing him to come in, to help you navigate painful memories, and to bring healing to your emotional wounds.

If you are dealing with some of the deepest wounds imaginable — marital betrayal, divorce, domestic violence, or spiritual, emotional, or sexual abuse — this exercise can be particularly challenging, but it also holds out the possibility of profound healing. In those situations, it may be best to ask a priest or a therapist to guide you, one who shares your Christian convictions about forgiveness and your decision to forgive your perpetrator.

Whatever the nature of your wounds and the forgiveness that you want to give, don't forget to have recourse to Our Lady who, as the ultimate example of all virtues, can teach us from her own experience. She undoubtedly experienced grave offenses and hurts, and she saw the Romans torture and brutally murder her innocent and flawless Son. And she forgave. Our Lady of Sorrows, pray for us!

Chapter 8
Going Even Deeper

Forgiveness as Prayer and Worship

*In the Judeo-Christian tradition, the primary act of
sacrifice is forgiveness.*

— *Roger Scruton*

We hope you've found the stories of forgiveness, the reflection questions in the first five chapters, the four-step process of forgiveness, and all the other information we've packed into this book so far helpful and healing. In this chapter, we invite you to go deeper. What if, with God's grace, you could embrace forgiveness as a daily spiritual practice? What if you were to discover that forgiveness can become prayer, can constitute a profound form of worship, and can set you on the fast-track to holiness?

Daily Forgiveness Exercise

In chapters 6 and 7, we provided a framework for prayerfully applying the four-step process of forgiveness to significantly hurtful experiences in your life. It is so important to address these major events and seek freedom from deep, underlying, entrenched unforgiveness. However, there are other types of hurts and other degrees of unforgiveness, less blatant, less deep, that we experience on a daily basis, and that we would do well to address.

We seem to be confronted with regular opportunities to hold a grudge. Sometimes such opportunities come out of nowhere and hit us like a sucker punch. Think, for example, of the verbal bombs that sometimes come our way. This can happen when we're having an otherwise pleasant conversation and somehow, suddenly, it spirals into unexpected territory. In her book, *You Can Share the Faith*, Karen Edmisten shares a great example of the off-hand but devastating remark that, without forgiveness, can cause resentfulness and unforgiveness to burrow in and fester:

> Years ago, just two weeks after I'd had my fifth miscarriage, I was at a gathering and met a friend's mother. She asked if I had children. At the time I had two, and I proudly shared my daughters' names and ages. She nodded politely and then turned to the woman next to me, who said she had five children. My friend's mother broke into an enormous smile. "That's *wonderful!*" she gushed. "So few people have that many these days!"

She didn't mean to be unkind, but I was devastated. Feeling fragile and defective, I wanted to shout, "I have more babies in heaven — don't they *count*?" She had no idea what I'd been through and, of course, it was not the time or place to recount my losses so I said nothing. But her words, born of assumptions, stung.

Karen did a good job of stepping back from the conversation and establishing a sense of perspective — the woman didn't know she had hurt Karen, would not have knowingly hurt her, and was in fact coming from what Karen described as "a good Catholic place," that is, the woman valued children and family life. In her mind, Karen forgave the woman almost instinctively. Nevertheless, she ultimately had to get beyond an intellectual understanding of the situation and her initial forgiveness. "It's one thing to understand why someone did something, and to forgive them, but often we still have to pray our way through to genuine forgiveness," Karen said. [1]

My (Dr. Lock's) experience with a pushy salesman is another example of the sort of less blatant irritants we encounter daily. I went to a furniture store to buy a chair for my office, and the salesman was a fast-talking, pushy guy. He presented lots of options that he insisted I *needed* for my office, to go with my chair. In actuality, I only needed the chair. Nevertheless, he pushed his agenda and wasted my time showing me items that were superfluous.

At the end of the day, I realized that I needed to forgive him for not listening to my request for a chair (and nothing else), for wasting my time, and for treating me like an object (a means to a paycheck) rather than a subject (a human person).

We have talked about the four-step forgiveness exercise and the whole-life forgiveness exercise. Now we'll introduce you to the daily forgiveness exercise so that you can apply the

Daily forgiveness will also strengthen the habit of forgiveness so that you can more readily and easily forgive. Otherwise, even these little experiences of hurt can compound and foster a general feeling of anger or agitation.

four steps of forgiveness to the little situations that occur on a daily basis. Doing so will help you resist the bondage of unforgiveness that can develop from even minor irritations. Daily forgiveness will also strengthen the habit of forgiveness so that you can more readily and easily forgive. Otherwise, even these little experiences of hurt can compound and foster a general feeling of anger or agitation. If life experiences are like water coming through a faucet, these little hurts are like hair in the drain that builds until the sink eventually backs up.

The daily forgiveness exercise can be done at any time of day, but it might work best for most people at the end of the day. The exercise is simple and will be familiar to you based on the previous chapters. You consider your day and where you have been offended, misunderstood, slighted, or otherwise hurt. If unforgiveness lurks in any of those situations, you intentionally, purposefully, and sincerely take each one individually into the four-step forgiveness process.

While my unpleasant encounter with the salesman was a minor incident in my day, without the daily forgiveness exercise

I might have walked around with a chip on my shoulder. When I reviewed my day, however, I recalled the situation (step 1) and quickly decided that I did want to forgive him (step 2). Then I prayed and told the Lord that I forgave him. I asked the Lord to forgive him, too, and finally I asked the Lord to pour out blessings upon him, his sales, his furniture store, and his family (step 3).

After my prayer, I went to sleep peacefully. Sometime the next day I thought about his financial situation, and I wondered if he was having trouble making ends meet. Another perspective that crossed my mind was that some people like a variety of accessories along with their furniture, but my tastes are more minimalist. I wondered if my pushy salesman was inclined to have lots of pretty side pieces of furniture and was making recommendations based on his preferences, not mine. All these reflections helped me to deepen my forgiveness toward him (step 4) and allowed me to more completely let go of resentment or irritation.

It sounds as if this daily forgiveness exercise could take a lot of time out of your day, but we have found that this is not the case. Regardless, every evening as you review the day, you will get better and better at spotting incidents of unforgiveness, and you will become more adept at walking through the four steps of forgiveness. You will discover, as you forgive the minor irritations of the past twenty-four hours, that you will become freer to completely engage in the experiences of the next twenty-four hours.

Examen Prayer and the Daily Forgiveness Exercise

If you have incorporated into your life the extremely salutary spiritual practice of the *examen prayer*, then you already have a sense of how a daily brief spiritual exercise of forgiveness can fit rather naturally into this practice. It is beyond the scope of this book to offer more than a very brief sketch of the examen prayer; fortunately, others have blessed the Church with more extensive and user-friendly guides to this wonderful practice.[2]

The examen prayer, as it is typically referred to, employs the Latin noun *examen*, meaning "examination." Having its origin in the Spiritual Exercises of St. Ignatius of Loyola,[3] the examen involves dedicating a short space of time — typically, although not necessarily, at the end of the day — to a spiritual self-examination. It has five steps, but we do not have to follow these in strict order. After recollecting myself in the presence and love of the Trinity:

1. I thank the Trinity for so many graces and blessings received throughout the period of time since my previous examen.

2. I ask for light and assistance to illumine my conscience and heighten my self-knowledge in the light of God's love.

3. I open myself to the light of the Holy Spirit, consider both the consolations (peace, light, insight, good choices, and actions made prompted by the Holy Spirit) and the desolations of my day (the negative emotions, fears, anxieties, sadness, and moral weakness). I then take a step back to look at my recent past in the light of faith. I look not merely for my failures or sinfulness, but more importantly for the movements and prompting of the Holy Spirit, and how I have been, or failed to be, docile to those inspirations.

4. I then allow our Lord to lead me to experience my own littleness, my creatureliness, as I rest in the gaze of the Father and his unconditional love for me, and express my sorrow for the ways I have failed to correspond to such an amazing love. I then formulate a resolution for the coming day.

5. I end by asking God for the grace to carry out that
    resolution in the coming day.

How does a daily exercise of forgiving others become part of
this dynamic? Let's go back to Karen's example and imagine her
doing the examen prayer one evening. After thanking our Lord
for some of the blessings received during the day and asking
for his light, she begins to recollect her day. As she does, she
realizes that something's been a little off in her interior. Then
she recalls that, as she was sipping her coffee in the morning,
the memory of the unpleasant encounter with her friend's
mother came back to her — even though several weeks had
passed since it had happened. She now sees that the memory
had been like a dark cloud hanging over her the whole day;
it was the source of the vague sense of sadness (desolation)
she had been experiencing. And she now sees that the memory
revived feelings of resentment and unforgiveness within her.
She also recalls that even though she quickly and instinctively
forgave the woman at the time, she knew her forgiveness would
need to go deeper.

So once again, she chooses to forgive her. She does so intentionally, praying for her by name, pronouncing the forgiveness specifically for her dismissive attitude, or lack of enthu-
siasm for Karen's two children, and her insensitivity. To help
deepen this act, she spends a couple of minutes recalling how
unintentional the woman's reaction was, and how she had no
way of knowing of Karen's miscarriages. She then moves on to
review other aspects of her day and conclude her examen.

Whether as part of the examen prayer, or simply as a daily
spiritual practice of its own, the daily forgiveness exercise is a
key means of deepening forgiveness over time, of "praying our
way through to genuine forgiveness" as Karen so aptly puts it.

Examining for Self-Forgiveness

It goes without saying that from time to time, whether as part of examen prayer or a daily exercise in forgiveness, we might become aware that unforgiveness of ourselves is the cause of some spiritual desolation we might be experiencing. As we uncover this in our self-examination, we can take the opportunity to ask for the grace, then and there, to open ourselves more radically to the reality of God the Father's forgiveness — perhaps already received sacramentally in confession.

In making a deliberate act of self-forgiveness, we should proclaim it in prayer as we saw in step 3. And standing firmly in our deep knowledge of the Father's unconditional love, we can simultaneously lay claim to a deeper interior freedom, calling on the name of Jesus:

> Lord Jesus, in your name, and aware of how uncondi-tionally and wonderfully I am loved by the Trinity, I renounce unforgiveness toward myself. In your name, Lord, I forgive myself for [_____].
> Since I have received your forgiveness and because I trust in your infinite mercy and goodness, I relinquish any and all self-loathing, and self-hatred, and I once again claim my freedom as beloved of my Father in heaven.

Such an act, under the influence of grace, can return us to a place of deeper interior freedom. From that freedom, we'll be on much better footing to respond responsibly and lovingly to those circumstances and relationships that our faults contin-ue to impact, even though we have sought self-forgiveness for those faults. Once I have received sacramental forgiveness, and have allowed myself to experience self-forgiveness, I can act with renewed interior freedom in those situations where my failings have harmed others. And I can contribute meaningfully to further reconciliation and reparation.

Forgiving from an Awareness of Our Own Sinfulness

"Let the one among you who is without sin be the first to throw a stone." — John 8:7

My honest awareness of my own sinfulness can be a great help in the process of forgiving others. When I am aware of my own failings, shortcomings, and sinfulness, when I consider *how I have hurt* others, then I am quite simply more easily disposed to forgive others. It seems to spiritually grease the process of forgiveness when I face the ways I have hurt others, or my consistent, even characteristic, failures in charity for which I must again and again ask the Father's forgiveness and the forgiveness of others — my spouse, my children, my peers:

> Why do you notice the splinter in your brother's eye, but do not perceive the wooden beam in your own eye? How can you say to your brother, "Let me remove that splinter from your eye," while the wooden beam is in your eye? You hypocrite, remove the wooden beam from your eye first; then you will see clearly to remove the splinter from your brother's eye. (Matthew 7:3–5)

The Desert Fathers recount a story of Abba Bessarion the Great, wonderworker of Egypt (d. 466): One day a priest became aware of a brother who had sinned gravely. So the priest kicked that brother out of the church. Observing this, Abba Bessarion got up and went with the brother saying, "I, too, am a sinner." This story illustrates the simple, powerful truth we're

> *The more acutely aware I am of my own sinfulness, the more ready I am to forgive, and the more easily and promptly I will do so.*

discussing: The more acutely aware I am of my own sinfulness, the more ready I am to forgive, and the more easily and promptly I will do so.

Pope Francis often speaks of forgiveness, including forgiving others, from the perspective of our own brokenness and sinfulness. In his apostolic visit to Santa Cruz-Palmasola Rehabilitation Center in Bolivia in July 2015, Pope Francis stood before a crowd of inmates who welcomed him affectionately:

> You may be asking yourselves: "Who is this man standing before us?" I would like to reply to that question with something absolutely certain about my own life. The man standing before you is a man who has experienced forgiveness. A man who was, and is, saved from his many sins. That is who I am.

The Holy Father reflected on this experience in the book *The Name of God Is Mercy*:

> The Pope is a man who needs the mercy of God. I said it sincerely to the prisoners of Palmasola, in Bolivia, to those men and women who welcomed me so warmly. I reminded them that even Saint Peter and Saint Paul had been prisoners.
>
> I have a special relationship with people in prisons, deprived of their freedom. I have always been very at-

tached to them, precisely because of my awareness of being a sinner. Every time I go through the gates into a prison to celebrate Mass or for a visit I always think: Why them and not me? I should be here. I deserve to be here. Their fall could have been mine. I do not feel superior to the people who stand before me. And so, I repeat and pray: Why him and not me?[4]

And noting how this sense of our own fragility and sinfulness can fuel our forgiveness of others, Francis said, in a general audience in Rome in 2020:

We're all indebted. All. To God, who is so generous, and to our brothers and sisters. Every person knows that he or she is not the father or mother they should be, the husband or wife, the brother or sister that they should be. We are all "deficient" in life. And we need mercy. We know that we too have done evil, there is always something missing from the good that we should have done.

But it is precisely this poverty of ours that becomes the force for forgiveness! We are indebted and if, as we heard at the beginning, we will be measured by the extent to which we measure others (cf. Luke 6:38), then we should enlarge the measure and pay back the debts, forgive. Everyone must remember that they need to forgive, we need forgiveness, we need patience; this is the secret of mercy: by forgiving you are forgiven.

Therefore, God precedes us and forgives us first (cf. Rm 5:8). By receiving his forgiveness, we become capable in turn of forgiving. Thus one's own misery and lack of justice become an opportunity to open up to the kingdom of heaven, to a greater measure, the measure of God, which is mercy.[5]

In his essay "Forgiveness," Fr. George Aschenbrenner helps us to unpack what this interior sense of our own sinfulness really is. Paradoxically, we are not talking about a sense of guilt that arises as we go, laundry-list style, through an accounting of our recent moral failures. Here, as Pope Francis alluded to above, we are talking about something much deeper, born first and foremost from our own sense of spiritual poverty, of our creatureliness, and of our absolute dependence on God. Aschenbrenner explains:

> Our sinfulness is not something we can become aware of all by ourselves if we put our mind to recalling past failures. Too often, this is where we look for our own sense of sin. God, however, must *reveal* to us our sinfulness. There is no other way to come to it. In the light of His love for us, our sinfulness is revealed.
>
> Many times, when we pray carefully about our Father's uniquely personal love for us, a kind of uneasiness begins to stir in our hearts. This can be the beginning of the revelation of sinfulness. ... Such an awareness is not received through an introspective moralistic examination of conscience. We need to be more reverently and humbly aware of the intimacy and depth of detail of His love for us rather than to stir up our own guilt-laden anxiety over past failures.
>
> If we really could know how much God loves us, we would be intensely aware in sorrow of our sinfulness! To stand openly in the light of His love will touch off in our hearts the shame, embarrassment, and sorrow of a sinner.[6]

It is from this awareness of our own spiritual poverty that a lifelong attitude of forgiveness can spring, and our readiness to forgive others can even become a form of giving worship to the living God.

Forgiveness as Prayer and Worship

In Saint Paul's well-known anthem to Christian charity (agape-love) in 1 Corinthians 13, he observes in verse 5 that "[charity] does not brood over injury." Infused charity disinclines us to dwell on the harms done to us and draws the Christian disciple to let go of resentment and unforgiveness. Agape-love draws us to a place of interior freedom and forgiveness.

This leads us to conclude the present chapter by considering something kind of extraordinary in the Christian life: Forgiveness can be a *genuine form of prayer and worship.*

Worship means giving honor and glory to God through various acts. Liturgical worship is obviously at the very heart of the worship we give God. The Church understands the Eucharist to be the "source and summit of Christian life" (LG, 11). Yet liturgical worship does not exhaust the manifold ways that we can give honor and glory to God. In fact, if liturgical worship does not give rise to a vibrant and virtuous gift of self to others, then something would be amiss within us spiritually.[7]

Forgiveness can be a genuine form of prayer and worship.

We can connect forgiveness and prayer because, at its core, to forgive someone in Christ is to bless them: blessing not in the sense of approval, but in its essential meaning of wanting and willing that the other receive all good things in God.

This is why, when people share with me (Father Tom) that they are struggling with forgiveness, I often simply ask: "Do you, right now, in your heart, want this person to receive every good thing now and in the life to come?" To actually will *that* and *mean it* is like a very trustworthy litmus test for whether I have truly forgiven someone who has hurt me. And to will this is, in

every sense, to bless this individual. In this sense, forgiveness is
a petition to God to bring every good gift into the life of the
perpetrator. And such a prayer gives great glory to God. It is to
begin to live a life of beatitude here on earth by living the new
life Jesus has given us:

> You have heard that it was said, "You shall love your
> neighbor and hate your enemy." But I say to you,
> love your enemies, and pray for those who persecute
> you, that you may be children of your heavenly Father,
> for he makes his sun rise on the bad and the good, and
> causes rain to fall on the just and the unjust. For if you
> love those who love you, what recompense will you
> have? Do not the tax collectors do the same? And if you
> greet your brothers only, what is unusual about that? Do
> not the pagans do the same? So be perfect, just as your
> heavenly Father is perfect. (Matthew 5:43–48)

Yet such choices — to love our enemies, to do good to those who
harm us, to forgive — such acts, Jesus teaches, are the very heart
of the "true worship" the Father desires (Jn 4:23). Such acts are
worship. Such acts are very truly liturgical, part and parcel of a
Christian life lived to the full in which our moral life, our life
of pursuing moral perfection, reaches its fullest extension and
expression in worship.[8]

What an amazing possibility! Every time we forgive others
in Christ, aided by grace, we offer true worship to God:

> Christian prayer extends to the *forgiveness of enemies*,
> transfiguring the disciple by configuring him to his
> Master. Forgiveness is a high-point of Christian prayer;
> only hearts attuned to God's compassion can receive the
> gift of prayer. Forgiveness also bears witness that, in our

world, love is stronger than sin. The martyrs of yesterday and today bear this witness to Jesus. Forgiveness is the fundamental condition of the reconciliation of the children of God with their Father and of men with one another. (*Catechism of the Catholic Church*, 2844)

Every act of such forgiveness moves us further along the high road to genuine holiness. And the possibilities are breathtaking. With God's grace, we can set out on this road to the heights of love, to the heights of peace with our neighbor, and of communion with the Trinity. On this road, he will continue to guide us to live in a state of forgiveness, re-forgiving when necessary, and genuinely loving those who have offended us — all in the footsteps of the Master.

Chapter 9
Saying "I Forgive You"

The Possibility of Reconciliation

*A stiff apology is a second insult. ... The
injured party does not want to be compensated
because he has been wronged; he wants to
be healed because he has been hurt.*

— G. K. Chesterton

Once we have worked through the four-stage process of forgiveness, we experience a certain release of negative emotions. Our lived experience is confirmed by research which shows us that after forgiveness, levels of anger, resentment, and bitterness decrease, as do tendencies toward depression and anxiety. By the same token, levels of happiness and contentment increase.

This business of forgiveness is such an intense interior experience. We truly labor in our mind and heart through the process of uncovering, deciding, proclaiming, and deepening. After spending so much energy "in our head," and experiencing the freedom of forgiveness, we may feel compelled to express this externally. We want to *say* something. And naturally, we want to say something to the individual with whom we have spent so much time in the inner workings of our mind and heart.

We want to say out loud, "I forgive you." Psychologically, that impulse makes perfect sense: It is helpful to make external what is happening internally. It is helpful to verbally articulate the silent inner workings of our mind and heart. Expressing this to the person allows for a certain closure. So a big part of us just wants the circle to be complete: I was hurt, I forgave, and the offender knows it, and now I want to say the magic words, "I forgive you." Then the conflict will be resolved, and we'll live happily ever after. Right?

We only wish it were as simple as that.

How exactly do you tell the person who hurt you, "By the way, I forgive you"? We'll come back to that at the end of this chapter. But let's note right off the bat that saying "I forgive you" is often dicey. Especially if the one who hurt you doesn't even know that his actions have hurt you. Are there ever times when it is appropriate to say, "I forgive you," for example, when no apology is offered? Let's just say, it depends! It depends on a lot.

Remember the story of Immaculée in the introduction? Immaculée returned to her Rwandan village, located the man who murdered her mother and brother, and said to him, "I forgive you." We have heard of other instances where the victim has approached the offender and forgiven him or her in this same style. Such an action is bold and beautiful, but it requires intense discernment. In preparing to make such a statement, the victim also has to be prepared for the situation to go poorly. We are also aware of situations where the victim has been shamed, screamed at, and silenced. The victim has to be prepared for an adverse reaction from the offender that could stir up a whole host of negative reactions within the victim. The last thing we want to see is revictimization of the one attempting to offer forgiveness.

With our closest friends and family members, however, saying "I forgive you" before the other has apologized can be fruitful if we are prepared to explain how we were hurt and what the other did, or failed to do, that offended us. Of course, here too we have to be prepared for the worst response, which will only add salt to a wound. The hope, however, is that we hear the best response, one where the offender realizes their misbehavior and repents. Regardless of the result, this conversation might be a little awkward to say the least, and it might end at a place we didn't expect.

Sometimes an explanation from the offender about the behavior could lead us to consider if our reaction was overly sensitive. Other times, the explanation could sound defensive, and we may need to explain why we still feel hurt. The key is to enter this discussion with an open heart and mind, and with goodwill toward the other. A close friendship can usually absorb the normal bumps and bruises of everyday interpersonal life. If you are unsure how to proceed, consult a trusted friend, priest, or mental health professional.

We hope that what follows can help you navigate the difficult waters related to verbally offering forgiveness, because the desire to express this forgiveness is, nevertheless, very real and healthy.

We've all hurt someone else. We've all been there.

So before we present the best approach to attempting to say, "I forgive you," we'd like to pivot to a brief exploration of the contents of an apology. To do this, it might be easiest to look at what we might do when we realize that *we* have hurt another person. We're going to take off the "I was hurt" shoes and put on the shoes of "I hurt someone." We've all hurt someone else. We've all been there. When we do realize that we offended someone, how do we say, "I am sorry"?

What's in an Apology?

An apology is not simply a gesture whereby we're looking to obtain forgiveness. When we approach another to apologize, we're seeking more than that. We're seeking reconciliation. What's the difference?

First, we'd like to state clearly that forgiveness is not the same as reconciliation. Forgiveness is the act of the will whereby we let go of our need for validation from the wrongdoer. Reconciliation is the explicit endeavor to restore friendship and harmony. The logical upshot, then, is that we can forgive someone without there being full reconciliation. Forgiveness is a first and necessary step toward reconciliation, but by itself, forgiveness is not yet reconciliation. So if we are reconciled, we have forgiven, but if we forgive, we are not necessarily reconciled.

Let's say this another way. Although we may forgive the individual who offended us, that relationship might still remain broken or at least wounded. You can forgive someone in your mind and heart, but you might not experience a healing of your relationship. Why? Because healing a relationship usually requires both parties to engage each other. Forgiveness is a condition for reconciliation, and sets the stage for it, but reconciliation requires another level of work after forgiveness. Reconciliation requires both parties to work to restore what was lost through the offense.

Here's an example. Our friends — we'll call them Bob and John — are psychologists in a nearby state. They have been friends since childhood and often play practical jokes on each other. These can be very funny, but about a decade ago, one got out of hand. Bob went on an online doctor review site and posted a negative comment — posing as one of John's clients — saying that John shared his personal information on social media without his permission. John found out because he met with a new client, who asked if the story they read on the review site was true. Ultimately, when John read the comment, he knew immediately that it was Bob. John called Bob to confront him, but the call went to voicemail. John left a livid message demanding that Bob delete the comment and call him back immediately. Later that evening, Bob sent John the following text: "Hey, yeah. Sorry dude. Was just trying to be funny. I hope you forgive me."

This apology was wildly insufficient; not at all proportionate to the offense committed. In fact, Bob didn't even acknowledge what the offense was! This informal "apology" lacked any regret, remorse, or sorrow. It even switched the responsibility for rectifying the situation from Bob to John ("I hope you forgive me"). This is hardly a true apology.

In a friendship, both individuals are responsible for the upkeep and maintenance of the friendship. When one friend hurts another, an apology and an effort to seek reconciliation are both in order. The friend who hurt the other, however, is responsible for fixing the problem that they created.

In this example, Bob was responsible for fixing the problem — and there were multiple problems. Bob needed to confront the fact that he allowed his attempt at humor to go way too far, leading him to discredit John. Further, Bob needed to self-reflect to understand if there were other motives behind the "humor" that motivated this level of defamation (today, many years later, we can confirm that there were). Figuring out those motivations was Bob's responsibility. He needed to look into himself to understand where this was coming from and why he did such a harmful thing. Writing bad stuff about John online falls under the heading of cyber-libel, a serious offense designed to undermine an individual's reputation through written statements. This misbehavior was also Bob's responsibility. In his apology, Bob didn't offer any suggestions for how he would counteract the lies he had spread about John. To offer a true apology, justice required that Bob take responsibility for what he did, explain why he acted as he did, and explain the steps he would take to ensure that this wouldn't happen again. Simply saying "Sorry, dude" doesn't suffice.

As we said, in a friendship both individuals are responsible for the upkeep of the relationship. As the one who hurt the other apologizes, the friend who was hurt works on forgiving. When the offended person accepts the apology and forgives the offender, the offender works at understanding where the offense came from and resolves never to repeat it.

Making an Effective Apology
Most people don't have a clear sense of how to make a substantial apology. We have a model for this process, however, in the Act of Contrition that we pray in the Sacrament of Reconciliation as a way to formally apologize to God. This little prayer captures a tremendous amount of the "good stuff" intrinsic to making an apology. We'll unpack it now to show how you can apply the formula of this prayer to making an apology to a friend

or family member.

Even though many of us may know the prayer by heart, let's read it through before we begin. Read it slowly and thoughtfully, considering the meaning of each part:

The Act of Contrition

O my God, I am heartily sorry for having offended Thee,
and I detest all my sins, because I dread the loss of heaven, and the pains of hell;
but most of all because they offend Thee, my God,
who are all good and deserving of all my love.
I firmly resolve, with the help of Thy grace,
to confess my sins, to do penance, and to amend my life.
Amen.[1]

In the sections that follow, we will *unpack* this prayer, a few words at a time, to better understand it, and then we'll *apply* each part to making an apology to a friend or family member.

O my God ...

Unpack: The prayer begins with "O" — the archaic form of "Oh." It can be found in Shakespeare, in the King James Bible, in the poetry of Keats, and elsewhere as a means of introducing an invocation. Often used to begin prayer, it expresses a heart crying out to the Lord. In the Act of Contrition, the O invocation invites the penitent to break from the path of sin, to burst forth in an apology and a plea for mercy. The next part names the One the prayer is addressing: my God.

Apply: It would be overly dramatic to use the "O" invocation in an apology, so we advise against that. However, addressing the individual by name is an important piece of an apology. It communicates respect and reverence for the offended person's dignity, and it's a powerful way to get their attention. An effective apology is not a general comment, but a specific statement, formulated for a specific person.

I am heartily sorry for having offended Thee ...

Unpack: The prayer continues with an expression of regret for the wrong we have done, as well as recognition of the hurt that we caused.

The responsibility lies with the apologizer, not with the one receiving the apology.

Apply: Both of these ideas — regret and recognition that we have injured the other person — are essential to an apology. We want to say that we are sorry. We also want to acknowledge the hurt that we caused. The first word in this line of the prayer is "I." Here we are accepting responsibility. "I" am saying that "I am the one who hurt you." The responsibility lies with the apologizer, not with the one receiving the apology. It's not an "I regret that I upset you." It's not an "I'm sorry, but ..." or "I hurt you, but ..." There is no deflection, no defensiveness, no shifting of blame.

As for the word "sorry," admittedly it's somewhat overused in our culture. If we greet someone who just lost a family member, we may say, "I'm sorry for your loss." If someone says they lost their job, we might say, "I'm so sorry." If someone tells us, "I was working in my garden and I got poison ivy," we might respond, "I'm sorry to hear that." In England it's common to say "sorry" when you don't hear or understand something someone said.

So what do we mean in our apology when we say "sorry"? We're speaking of remorse: "I am pained because what I did (or failed to do) hurt you." I am "heartily" sorry. My "sorry" is substantial, and it weighs on my heart.

The next part of this line in the prayer is "for having offended Thee." While that's too formal for the average conversation, we might say "for having hurt you" or, even better, by naming the specific offense, for example, "for having disregarded you" or "for having failed to be there for you when you needed me." In so doing, we are taking responsibility for our behavior.

And I detest all my sins ...

Unpack: We acknowledge, in this line of the prayer, that we dislike our behavior and, even more clearly, that our behavior was sinful.

Apply: We underscore the genuineness of our apology when we express our disgust at our own hurtful behavior. We're saying that our behavior was inappropriate, not just in this situation, but in any situation in which we sin against others. We detest, we hate, we abhor our hurtful behavior. And when we detest something, we don't want to do it again.

Because I dread the loss of heaven, and the pains of hell; but most of all because they offend Thee, my God, who are all good and deserving of all my love.

Unpack: This line of the prayer expresses our remorse or our guilt — and our fear of losing the God we love. The fear of hell can move us to avoid sin, but here the Act of Contrition instills in us a deeper, more genuine motive for renouncing sin: love for our God who is all good and, therefore, deserving of love and not offense. We express tenderness toward God here, from hearts all too aware of our own brokenness.

Apply: When we hurt another, we want to acknowledge that our behavior has had a negative impact on them; we want to acknowledge the hurt. We also note that the other person doesn't deserve our offensive behavior. Given the inherent dignity of the person, they deserve our respect and reverence.

I firmly resolve, with the help of Thy grace, to confess my sins, to do penance, and to amend my life.

Unpack: At the end of the Act of Contrition, we make a commitment to change our lives in order to demonstrate, not only with our words, but with our actions, that we are deeply sorry. We make a resolution. A firm one! We acknowledge that change can only take place with the Lord's help. We promise to be honest, to make up for the sin committed, and to alter our future conduct.

Apply: An effective apology includes a promise to avoid that behavior in the future. Sometimes this can be simply stated; other times you will need to offer a more detailed explanation of how you plan to change your life.

In an interpersonal relationship, we would translate the prayer's commitment "to do penance" as a commitment "to repair." This implies an immediate repairing of the wrong, in addition to future improvements. How can the apologizer fix the wrong he has done? Sometimes the apologizer sees a clear path forward. Other times, the apologizer will have to ask the one offended what they want or need from the apologizer in order to address the harm and start the healing process.

Paul and Julie and the Art of the Apology

Paul's timing couldn't have been worse. He sold his successful limousine business and opened a restaurant right before the COVID-19 pandemic hit. He lost the restaurant within six months and, feeling horribly dejected, started an entry-level career in sales. His salary was well below what he had previously earned, but it was a regular paycheck with benefits. Given the career difficulties, financial struggles, and stress, however, he soon became depressed. His wife, Julie, encouraged him to enter counseling with me (Dr. Lock).

As therapy unfolded, Paul disclosed that he and his wife

were experiencing difficulties, though he had trouble articulating what those were. At my suggestion, Paul invited Julie in for a few sessions, and she pretty quickly disclosed the nature of their problem. Julie shared that Paul often said inappropriate things of a sexual nature to her and about her in front of their children. Paul didn't think there was anything wrong in what he said, but Julie was disgusted.

In subsequent sessions, Paul talked about his upbringing and his understanding of the dignity of women. He grew up in a rough neighborhood where men often spoke of women in a derogatory way. He felt that the way he talked to Julie was nothing compared to what he heard growing up. Gradually in our sessions, however, he began to understand not only that he had a distorted view of women, but also that his comments were demeaning and disordered. No wonder Julie was offended. He realized, too, that he was modeling negative behavior for his children.

In between sessions, Paul told Julie he was sorry, but this enraged her: How could that make up for years of damage? Julie sent him back to therapy to learn how to make a proper apology.

Together, Paul and I explored the idea of developing an apology based on the structure of the Act of Contrition. Paul liked this idea because it gave him a road map to walk through the apology. Nevertheless, it was challenging because he knew that he would have to work hard to stop making these comments which, by this point in his life, were automatic.

He wrote his apology down in preparation, but he didn't read it to her. (Sometimes clients do read their apology letter when the time is right.) Paul simply kept in mind his talking points. Here's what he wrote:

> Julie, I'm really sorry for having hurt you and been disrespectful toward you for so many years. I'm also really

sorry that I said those things in front of our kids. I hate that I have been disrespectful because it's wrong. Period. But also because it hurts you and it teaches the kids that this is OK even though it's not OK. No one deserves to be talked to that way.

I want to quit saying these things; I want to say things to you that build you up, not tear you down. I want my kids to know how to talk in a respectful way to their mother, and to any woman. I will be talking to the kids to tell them that I have realized my mistake. If you would like to be there when I talk to the kids, you're welcome to join us and add anything to the conversation. If you don't want to be there, that's fine and I will meet with them myself. I also will continue to explore this issue in counseling to be sure that I change my ways.

In a follow-up session, Paul reported that he made the apology, and that Julie didn't take it well. She felt sure he'd do it again. Paul expressed his own concern that he'd keep speaking disrespectfully, but then he shared his plan with Julie for how, through therapy and talking to a close friend and his parish priest, he hoped to make a significant change.

Julie didn't want to be present when he talked to the kids, so Paul spoke with them alone. That was also a difficult conversation because his kids accused him of trying to whitewash over his years of abusive comments. Paul understood their perspective, but he said that he could only start today and move forward.

A few months later, Julie reported that Paul showed real signs of change. There had been a few minor slips, but when Paul became aware of what he was saying, either by realizing it himself or by Julie pointing it out, he immediately corrected himself. Julie was convinced that Paul was making a big effort, and she was able, when she joined us in the therapy, to express how damaging his comments had been over the years. This was, again, very difficult for Paul to hear, and it took him some time to digest. As a man, he wanted to "do" something, but he learned from Julie that she just wanted him to hear her out and to continue on the road of correcting himself.

Dos and Don'ts of Effective Apologies

Paul and Julie's story offers many lessons, one of the most important of which is that we have to be real. Both the apologizer and the one receiving the apology need to be "authentic." Julie didn't feel Paul was sincere, and it was important that she shared this. Paul, for his part, had to grapple sincerely with his arrogance and pride. He shared in therapy that many times he reverted to his old ways of thinking. He sometimes wanted to say to Julie, "Get over it." But he didn't. Instead, he brought it to therapy, and we dug deep into his heart and mind. As he became more and more real with himself, he was able to recognize that in these moments, he was feeling the most acute shame from the damage he had caused. Forgiving himself allowed him to grow in freedom and to be nondefensive in the face of Julie's justified anger.

When receiving an apology, the receiver should hear sincerity in the words the apologizer uses to express regret and to take responsibility for the harm done. The receiver should also "feel" that the apology is sincere and be convinced that the apology addresses the heart of the offense. If the receiver doesn't feel this, they should be free to say that. Then the offender can reflect on his apology to revise the delivery to satisfy the receiver. The apology is about righting the wrong; it's about the person receiving the apology. The apology should, on some level, make the one offended feel better. An apology is *not* about the apologizer; it is *not* about making the apologizer "feel better" or relieved (even though, in reality, most times when we apologize, we *do* feel quite relieved).

> *The apology is about righting the wrong; it's about the person receiving the apology. The apology should, on some level, make the one offended feel better.*

The apology might develop into a dialogue in which the apologizer can learn more about the particular pains or injuries that must be addressed to heal the wound. The apologizer should make an effort to mute any defensiveness and, instead, work to make the apology real for the person offended. The apology is not about winning points, or crossing a finish line, much less about "getting it over with." An apology is about applying balm to a wound, not re-opening the wound.

Finally, and critically, the apologizer should avoid *asking* for forgiveness. When offering an apology, people often say things like, "Please forgive me" or "I hope you can forgive me" or "Do you accept my apology?" The problem with these is that they apply pressure on the one receiving the apology to accept it and move on. But sometimes it takes time to absorb the apology. Sometimes the one receiving the apology needs clarification before being ready to accept it. The apologizer should avoid pressuring the one receiving the apology and allow that individual whatever time they need to process it before responding.

Apology + Forgiveness = Reconciliation

Our deep dive into the art of apologizing should help us better understand when it's appropriate to say "I forgive you," and how to move toward reconciliation in order to restore a ruptured relationship.

The one doing the apologizing must take the lead on the road to reconciliation. This explains why reconciliation isn't always possible, even when we have forgiven the offender. It takes two to reconcile. Forgiveness is one enormous piece of the formula, but only one piece. Reconciliation will only be possible when the one apologizing takes up the responsibility of satisfying the one who was hurt. While the offended party can be the first to make a move — by deciding to forgive — reconciliation requires the offender to engage the offended. Reconciliation can only happen when the offender offers a genuine apology that the offended person can meet with genuine forgiveness.

Receiving an Apology and Saying "I Forgive You"

In the best-case scenario, the offender will realize that they have hurt you and approach with an effective apology. When someone approaches you to offer an apology, you should reverence that moment. This is a very delicate (and often awkward) experience.

Perhaps this is obvious, but the first step to receiving an apology is to listen. As much as possible, take a few moments alone and uninterrupted with the person apologizing so that you can clearly hear what they are saying. Focusing in this way will allow you to understand the heart of the offender. If they express humility, regret, and sorrow, you will hear that *and* feel that.

Next, ask questions. If you want something clarified, ask. If you are concerned about what the apologizer is saying, or if you want the offender to say more, be honest. Share your thoughts.

Then take time to reflect. Often, we feel compelled to accept an apology and move on, but by doing so, we may fail to reverence ourselves. We're not computers, we're people. And people take time to absorb and to process significant life events. It's reasonable to say, "Thank you for your apology. I need some time to absorb what you just said and then I'd like to talk about it a little more."

At some point, the offended person has to determine if the apology is acceptable. If the answer is no, this may prompt more dialogue with the offender. There may be some situations, particularly traumatic ones, that call for a longer dialogue or a series of discussions. For this type of conversation, it's often necessary that a third party, such as a priest or a therapist, lead the discussion.

Sometimes when an apology is not acceptable, the forgiver may come to realize that the offender isn't capable of offering an appropriate apology. It's sad, but unfortunately true, that many people aren't mature or healthy enough to take responsibility for their behavior and to see past themselves. This could be another wound that the injured party can take into the four-step forgiveness process, forgiving the offender for being unable to apologize.

If the apology is acceptable, then the forgiver can tell the apologizer, "I accept your apology." Furthermore, the forgiver can add, "and I forgive you." This is our definition of reconciliation: when a genuine apology is accepted and forgiveness is offered. Only then can a relationship be returned to a state of equality and homeostasis. In this situation, the relationship is restored. Now, truly, the circle is complete: I was hurt, I forgave, and the offender knows it. We have resolved the conflict arising from the hurt. Harmony is now restored, at least to some degree, the relationship is on the road to recovery, and reconciliation has blossomed.

Conclusion

This book has certainly not said all there is to say about forgiveness, but we've highlighted some elements that are particularly important and applicable to daily life. We hope the experience of working through these chapters — even prayerfully so — has been rewarding for you. Of course, the experiences and challenges of forgiveness offer a lifetime of learning. And while we never quite "graduate" or get to the end of that school of forgiveness, we hope that having worked through our book, you find yourself, by God's grace, at a real commencement: the beginning of a new project of life, in some sense, the life of being a more committed *forgiver*.

No doubt as you read through the preceding chapters, significant memories rose to the surface. We can only hope that your perseverance, even through reawakened feelings of resentment or anger, and your prayerful openness to grace as you progressed through these pages have nonetheless paid off. As you finish, however, you may be tempted to say, "That was a really nice book," but not let it *change your life*. We hope, however, that this book can have that kind of life-changing impact, giving you the steps to begin and continue the journey of forgiveness.

Finally, as you experience the benefits of embracing forgiveness, we encourage you to share your experience with others. Nothing is more evangelical than to hear a personal witness of how the Lord has made you free. When we hear stories of forgiveness in other people's lives, it inspires us to forgive in our own life. Who could hear Immaculée's story, for example, and not be compelled to examine their own heart? How could we hear of her heroic forgiveness and not realize: "I guess I can forgive my teenage son for getting a speeding ticket" or "I'm ready to forgive my old landlord for unjustly keeping the security deposit"?

Of course, as we have tried to express throughout the book, there are some very painful experiences that make forgiveness seem impossible. With deep wounds, we understand and we affirm the profound difficulty and strength and courage that it takes to apply the steps of forgiveness.

To be sure, forgiveness might at times seem unattainable, *unimaginable*, yet our prayer is that you won't push forgiveness away. Our prayer is that this book will help you open up to the possibility that forgiveness is *imaginable*. Our prayer, to be even more daring, is that you will deepen your trust in all that is possible with God's grace, that you will experience the Lord waiting to help you to grow more and more in the freedom he wants to give you.

So, let's not shy away from the bold, arduous, and healing journey of forgiveness, a journey we will need to undertake throughout our lives: exploring and uncovering the caverns of unforgiveness; crossing the valleys of shame, anger, and self-forgiveness; reaching the plateau of decision and proclaiming our choice;

plumbing the depths and going deeper; even ascending the summit of loving the one who has offended us. Time and again, if we are open to the workings of grace, these journeys will become immensely rewarding, transforming us "from glory to glory" (2 Cor 3:18).

Afterword
Can Forgiveness Help Heal a Hurting Church?

"Love is the greatest strength of the powerless. ... Love is all-powerful and will even overcome hatred. And only love can do this!"

— *Václav Havel*

It is our hope that, guided by grace, we might all embrace the call to meditate on, and unleash in our own life, the magnificent power of forgiveness in Christ. Forgiveness is a great wellspring of personal healing. It can repair shattered relationships; and as we have seen, it restores interior freedom to the one who has been hurt, and empowers victims of crime and abuse to recover the dignity and agency they were stripped of by the offender.

Since forgiveness restores interior freedom in an individual, can that somehow get bumped up to a more macro level? Is there a way to apply this to the healing of not just an individual, but a community? The simple answer is yes. However, this is not a simple endeavor.

Both authors are intensely committed to our faith, and both share a passion to help accompany survivors of clergy sexual abuse. Thus, a question flowing from the hearts of the authors: Can we help individuals heal and somehow fuel forgiveness in the greater Church?

Can Forgiveness Help Heal a Hurting Church?

It is our assumption that the vast majority of our readers are not indifferent to the Catholic Church's continuing struggle to be free of the scourge of sexual abuse in our midst. This has entailed the undertaking in recent decades of a herculean effort to transform a culture within the institutional Church that too often hid the crimes of abusers, wittingly or unwittingly enabled their abuse, and treated victims as litigants, not as hurting sons and daughters. Some of that has begun to change, but there is still a long, long way to go. It begins with a commitment to transparency on the part of the Church's hierarchy, and a determination not only that perpetrators be brought to justice whenever possible, but a readiness to accompany survivors of abuse for the long haul.

Every instance of sexual abuse in the Catholic Church — whether perpetrated by a priest, religious, or layperson — like detonating a bomb, has a devastating blast radius. Beyond the immediate victim, it devastates parents, siblings, and friends of both victim and perpetrator.

The sexual abuse crisis has also deeply impacted Catholics in the pew. And beyond the scandal and harm perpetrated by priest abusers who have lived double lives, the Church has been deeply wounded by the scandal of the Church's leadership, whose approach for decades, if not centuries, has been to hide the reality — in the name of "not causing further scandal."

The betrayal and anger experienced by the Catholic faithful hit a boiling point with revelations of the sickening rise to power of Theodore McCarrick and the blind eye turned by so many who had reason to suspect, or worse had positive knowledge of, his sexual predations.

In the wake of the McCarrick scandal, a veil has been lifted on a significant minority of sexually active priests; on a clerical culture of tolerance of sexual sin and of behavior that can easily become abusive; and on the twisted dynamic of perpetrators leveraging a power differential over their victims, whether minor or adult.

Beyond cynicism, these and other revelations have bred discouragement and despair among many members of the laity and the sense that the system is broken and beyond repair.

∾

If you have been hurt in the Church, whether as a victim of abuse or as a spectator of this unfathomable crisis, we would invite you to join us in a reflection meant to enkindle hope — hope that our Church, and the individuals so grievously impacted, can heal. Beyond your own struggles to forgive, we invite you now to turn your heart to the Church we love, the Church for whom we suffer, with whom we struggle, the Church so many of us serve in different capacities.

The Church's response to the crisis of clergy sexual abuse has not been uniform. Much more needs to happen in terms of pastoral ministry for victims in order to bring healing to the Church.

Beyond its programs instituting training in the protection of minors for anyone doing ministry with minors (offered in the United States, Canada, and parts of Europe, principally Ireland, France, and Germany), the wholesale adoption of a retributive approach to justice still leaves other dimensions of this crisis painfully neglected. While valid in its core premise that wrongdoing deserves consequences, retributive justice focuses on punishing the offender, often underemphasizing the need to assist and accompany the victim.

What we should learn from listening to victims of abuse is that the current ecclesial regime of training and protection protocols, essential norms for dealing with priest-offenders, and retributive justice for perpetrators — as important as these are — will never by themselves bring healing to the Church. We need a better approach.

Restorative Justice

For the past few decades, victim advocates and those most involved with survivors of abuse have been insisting that the Church's institutional outreach to victims must move beyond financial payments to real accompaniment. Survivors of abuse remind us over and over again: It's not about compensation, but compassion.[1] As Janine Geske and Stephen Pope have insisted so clearly:

> Making amends should not be reduced to making financial payments. Some members of the hierarchy do not understand that monetary compensation (however costly) is a necessary *but not sufficient* means to restoration and healing. A more expansive and Christlike commitment to *caritas* would help some bishops move beyond an overriding and morally blinding preoccupation with legal and financial liability.[2]

In this context, it is our conviction that to heal a hurting Church, we need to turn with greater energy, hope, and dedication to unleashing the power of forgiveness.

As the preceding chapters should make more than evident, however, it is hardly our intention to suggest that victims of abuse should forgive their perpetrators and "move on." Tragically, that too often has been the message received by survivors of abuse from clergy and laity alike — because it's the "Catholic thing to do." But such an approach to victims is, in fact, a grotesque caricature of genuine Christian love.

What is needed is an approach that seeks just retribution for perpetrators while at the same time restoring dignity and agency to victims. Many of us find hope in applying a *restorative justice* approach to the crisis of sexual abuse in the Church.

Restorative justice is typically defined as a process whereby all stakeholders in the offense come together to seek resolution, to deal with the aftermath of the offense and the future implications for all the stakeholders involved.[3] This process includes many dimensions: that the victim come face to face with the perpetrator so that the perpetrator might hear the victim's story, look the victim in the eye, and apologize; that the victim might have his or her agency and dignity restored by forgiving the perpetrator, and the perpetrator have the opportunity to commence a process of making amends; and often through this process, victims have the opportunity to discover empathy for the offender, recognizing him or her as neighbor, as brother or sister.

The aim is first and foremost about healing, for victim and perpetrator, and all those impacted by the offense.

Casey's Story

Casey was twenty-seven at the time of her abuse. Having recently experienced a powerful conversion, and still working through issues from her troubled upbringing, she was serving as a Catholic lay missionary. Her early experiences of the Faith were energizing, yet she was still very wounded — and altogether extremely vulnerable. It was in this context that a Catholic priest groomed her and eventually raped her. She was retraumatized and revictimized as Church officials behaved with incredulity and indifference, lacked empathy, and treated her as a cog in a process.

It took a few years before, finally, a caring diocesan attorney and a local priest became involved. Although the lawyer assured Casey that the diocese would pay for her therapy, it was clear that she was not interested in monetary rewards. At the encouragement of both, Casey courageously went public with her story. This prompted the Church to take more effective measures, including the attempt of a cardinal to ensure that this priest's bishop (the priest was from a diocese outside the United States) would undertake a canonical investigation. That investigation seems to have taken place — yet *to this day* the priest remains in ministry.

Casey's story is illustrative.

First, her experience highlights the sense of abandonment and emptiness in a victim's heart when a diocese takes a merely retributive approach to justice. That very approach, meant to remedy a wrong, does little to heal a heart.

Casey's journey also brought her to a deeper, personal understanding of the compatibility of forgiveness and justice. In personal correspondence with Father Tom, Casey shared how, over time, these graced insights came to her, beginning with the need to renounce her own desire for vengeance:

> I had a wise therapist who helped guide me through some of these feelings and as I began to process the trauma, some of the resentment began to fade. I realized that

the anger itself was not a sin, but rather what I did with the anger. It was freeing for me to realize that feelings are morally neutral; it is what we do with the feelings that matter. It allowed me to feel the feelings and process them without allowing them to control me.

This is not to say that we do not seek justice. I have heard prelates tell victims to "forgive and forget" the abuse, but this is a perversion of mercy. Justice and mercy are not contradictory. We must seek to expose sins and bring them to the light of Christ. We must also seek to bring criminals to justice for the sake of other potential victims but also for the sake of the perpetrator himself.

Casey's experience also teaches us, as she puts it so well, that "healing is not linear nor is forgiveness. It is a process that takes time." For those experienced in practices of restorative justice, this becomes more than evident. At the heart of these practices is the *healing circle*, in which, after sometimes years of preparation, victims, perpetrators, and other stakeholders come together, first and foremost to hear each other's stories. It is in this context that sorrow and repentance can be expressed, and forgiveness asked for and received.

Not surprisingly, it is in this context that a facile, superficial, or even false forgiveness comes to be distinguished from genuine forgiveness, the fruit of years of arduous and consistent effort by the victim to recover and sustain *an attitude of benevolence toward the perpetrator.* Within the practice of restorative justice, it becomes clearly evident how forgiveness is more like a way of life.

Casey's insight about the emotions that accompany the process of forgiveness should not be lost on us. In chapter 5 we explored the reality that, in the healing process of emotional wounds, we can find ourselves dealing — sometimes for years on end — with the most intense emotions, particularly anger. Anger, as we said earlier, is a legitimate and even reasonable reaction to moral hurt; and no less of an authority than St. Thomas Aquinas would agree with us on that.[4] It all depends on what we do with the anger: Do we allow it to control us, or do we grapple with it, finding healthy, constructive outlets for expressing it?

It all depends on what we do with the anger: Do we allow it to control us, or do we grapple with it, finding healthy, constructive outlets for expressing it?

In other words, love compels us to rightly channel our anger, but it does not require us necessarily to abandon anger prematurely. In the case of the most grievous harms — particularly for victims of sexual abuse — a relatively stable reaction of anger toward the perpetrator is not incompatible with forgiveness, especially in practices of restorative justice. Sometimes we need this anger residue to fuel the quest for justice which otherwise may lose steam as emotions fade and we become desensitized. Again, it is a matter of our gaining and sustaining control of that strong emotion, not to permanently live in this state, but in order to will the good of the perpetrator and — dare we say — to love the perpetrator.[5]

Emily's Story: Forgiveness as Redemptive Journey

Forgiveness in the context of the Church's sexual abuse crisis entails not only the forgiving of perpetrators. It can embrace, as well, what is sometimes for victims an equal or greater challenge: namely, to forgive those responsible for enabling the abuser, as well as those tasked with outreach to victims. For Emily Ransom, it was the latter of the two challenges that was most daunting and most painful. She shared her story in the June 2020 issue of *Church Life Journal*.[6] Emily, like so many victims, found the process of reporting her abuse, dealing with — in her case — the superiors of the religious community of which her perpetrator was a member, utterly retraumatizing, leaving deeper wounds than the abuse itself.

That retraumatization of victims, in and through the very bureaucratic processes supposedly intended to serve them, has sadly been the plight of far too many survivors of abuse. For Emily, it was excruciating. While well-intentioned ecclesiastical authorities were taking seriously the evil that had been done to her, they were failing to take seriously the good which she wanted to bring into this tragedy, namely, the gift of her forgiveness, and her hope that her perpetrator could recover his own dignity and wholeness. Upon engaging with those authorities, she immediately discovered that she was being sucked into a bureaucratic process that had no use for her gift. She was not to contact the perpetrator, she was not to be involved in whatever was next for him, and eventually she was told: "We will be in contact with you." That contact and communication with her perpetrator's religious superiors dried up after a few months. As far as Emily was concerned, the initial violence she suffered from her perpetrator was followed by violence from the institutional Church. The Church had rendered her gift, her forgiveness, ineffectual.

Emily's story, her candor and vulnerability, are especially remarkable because her abuse occurred as an adult. In publishing
her story, Emily understood that she was opening herself up to
what so many adult victims of abuse and sexual assault must
confront: victim blaming. Although thirty-five at the time, Emily
had never dated, and she was a very recent convert to Catholicism: both elements which predisposed her own naïveté with
regard to the man who eventually abused her, someone she considered, *and still considers*, to be a brother in Christ.

In going public with her story, it should be noted, she had
to confront what she calls the "dupe-factor" — namely, that any
victim who reports their abuse or goes public with their story
can struggle with feeling like a fool for having succumbed to the
perpetrator's grooming and overtures. This sensation of humiliation can constitute a real hurdle for many victims and may explain why it often takes so long for them to come forward.

She is grateful for the #MeToo movement for opening the
possibility for her to transcend her own confusion and come to
understand the complex reality of what had happened to her:

No, my friends insisted, I had not been "asking for it."
They pointed out the abused power dynamic between
a priest and a laywoman, between a host and his out-
of-town guest, of age and esteemed reputation on one
side and youth and early-career vulnerability on the
other. Yes, they maintained, legally it was sexual assault,
physical contact of a sexual nature without consent. No,
they clarified, my frightened inaction was absolutely not
consent, and consenting to one thing did not imply consenting to another; in the absence of active consent, it
was assault.

The #MeToo movement indeed led to a deeper public understanding of how abusers leverage their power to exploit their victims.[7] Yet Emily was not ultimately satisfied with the answers she was finding in the contemporary fixation on retributive justice. She was compelled to go deeper, to embark, as she describes it, on a journey seeking a "redemptive path" to turn what happened to her "into a story of hope."

Restorative Justice, the Crisis of Clerical Sexual Abuse, and the Triumph of Grace

Practices of restorative justice have a deep natural affinity to the restorative and redemptive possibilities of forgiveness in Christ. As we have seen in earlier chapters, grace builds on nature. In the Church's ongoing response to the sexual abuse crisis, we should be able to combine the best practices of restorative justice with a vibrant faith in the transforming power of grace and the deeply redemptive nature of forgiveness in Christ.

Emily's story wonderfully illustrates this.

First, her story brings into clear relief one of the deepest contributions from practices of restorative justice — namely, that forgiveness is an immensely positive and empowering act for victims of abuse. Reflecting with Father Tom on her experience now several years removed from the abuse, she shared in an email exchange:

> Forgiveness does something (heals, redeems, blazes a new trail, seeks the good), rather than only not doing something (not lashing out, not resenting, etc.). It's that negative understanding of forgiveness that can seem so damaging for victims of abuse. The crime itself had stripped their agency, and if forgiveness is understood as *not acting*, it does keep them in the position of passivity. But forgiveness understood positively was not only

comforting but also dignifying, restoring my agency and choosing to write something else over the story of destruction.[8]

At the very heart of practices of restorative justice in the context of the Church's sexual abuse crisis, forgiveness is conceived of as an extraordinarily *positive and empowering* action on the part of the victim, as Emily has just underlined. It presumes an attitude of benevolence toward the perpetrator, acknowledging him or her once again as *neighbor*. By the same token, forgiveness is compatible with just anger toward the offender, anger aimed ultimately at the offender's own good. It can accommodate both the remission of punishment or the administration of appropriate punishment for the good of all: the victim, the other stakeholders, and, again, the perpetrator. Forgiveness forgoes and withstands the inclination to hate the perpetrator and to seek revenge, and it can accommodate both the renunciation and the retention of feelings of resentment.

Yet Emily's journey brought her much further. It compelled her to bring her human readiness to forgive before the cross of Jesus, and there to plumb the depths of the mystical work and transformative power of the heart of Christ who takes our deepest hurts, our most brutal sufferings, and can make them redemptive:

I felt the paucity of the prior models available to me, especially at this particular historical moment that saw retributive justice as the primary alternative to sweeping offenses under the rug. To find an alternative, I thus shut out the voices of ... both the #MeToo movement and the call for reckoning in the clerical sexual abuse crisis. After all, this was my assault, not theirs. They were not yet asking the questions I needed, questions about healing,

redemption, forgiveness, reconciliation. For those questions, I could only turn to the Gospel.

Emily discovered there, in a deeply intimate and personal way,
how Jesus responds and what he says — in the today of our
Church — to the tragedy of the sexual abuse crisis. Jesus, the
Lord of life and of human history, can envelop darkness with
light, and can submerge sinfulness, betrayal, and our deepest
tragedies into a flood of grace. The wounds he bore in his hands,
feet, and side, even after the Resurrection, are the most eloquent
testimonial of this divine triumph:

> Christ's Passion is never erased, and Christ himself
> forever bears the wounds. It is not erased; it is transfig-
> ured by the resurrection when "death is swallowed up
> in victory" (1 Cor 15:54). The worst thing imaginable
> becomes the instrument of our redemption precisely
> because of its inalterable horror. Mysteriously, Christ
> invites my own suffering into a participation in this re-
> demptive act.

Only Christ can save his Church from the sexual abuse crisis. We
are called to be collaborators with him in this work of salvation.
Ours is to be sharers in what is surely already a lifetime struggle,
one encompassing this and the next generation. The practices of
restorative justice point us in a very good direction — what we
might call "Eucharistic justice," a portfolio of restorative practices that include truth-telling, acknowledging the suffering of survivors, the healing of memories, reparations, apologies, penance,
punishment, and forgiveness.[9]

Grace can work upon those efforts, sublimating and transforming them by the power of Jesus' resurrection: "Where, O
death, is your victory? Where, O death, is your sting?" (1 Cor

15:55). This is Christ's response to the abuse crisis.

And because of that, we have no reason to respond with anything less than a resilient hope for the healing of our Church, and a tender empathy for our brothers and sisters who have suffered so unspeakably. The powerful witness of Casey and Emily and so many other survivors of abuse who have traveled the rugged road of forgiveness refreshes our faith, enkindles our charity, and emboldens our hope.

Prayer to Mary, Mother of Forgiveness

Heavenly Father, in the name of Jesus, and by the power of the Holy Spirit, I ask for the willingness to forgive and the grace to forgive immediately all who have sinned against me. On Calvary, you gave Mary the grace to forgive me for my part in killing her Son. Then you gave Mary the grace to become my mother (Jn 19:26–27).

Mary, Mother of Forgiveness, may I forgive others as you forgave me in imitation of your Son. Mary, take my hand and lead me as I decide to accept God's grace to forgive (name the person) for (name the sin), etc.

Jesus, thank you for giving me Mary, "Mother of Forgiveness," to be my mother.

Mary, Mother of Forgiveness, pray for me.

Nihil obstat: Reverend Ralph J. Lawrence, July 8, 1997

Imprimatur: † Most Reverend Carl K. Moeddel, Vicar General and Auxiliary Bishop of the Archdiocese of Cincinnati, July 21, 1997

The prayer and a Novena to Mary, Mother of Forgiveness, can be found here: www.presentationministries.com

Notes

Introduction: So, Why Are You Reading this Book?

1. Immaculée Ilibagiza, *Left to Tell: Discovering God amidst the Rwandan Holocaust* (New York: Hay House, 2006), 196.

2. Ibid., 204.

3. Ibid., 93.

Chapter 1: Getting at the Root

1. David Konstan, in *Before Forgiveness: The Origins of a Moral Idea* (Cambridge University Press, 2010), has maintained that our contemporary understanding of forgiveness, so steeped in a sense of interpersonal relationships and the values attendant to those relationships, largely evolved in the modern era and was virtually unknown not only in the classical period, but even within Judaism and early Christianity:

> The notion of interpersonal forgiveness, as it is basically understood today, is not only not universal but also is of relatively recent coinage, and that the ancient societies to which we often look as models for our ethical concepts — whether classical Greece and Rome, or the Jewish and Christian traditions that emerged within and alongside them — seem to have done perfectly well without it. (170–171)

Such a conception would seem to entirely have missed not only the novelty of Christian forgiveness, but its deeply interpersonal nature from the get-go, as in Matthew 18:35: "So will my heavenly Father do to you, unless each of you forgives his brother *from his heart*" (ἀπὸ τῶν καρδιῶν ὑμῶν). Anthony Bash ("Did Jesus Discover Forgiveness?" *Journal of Religion Ethics*, 41:3 [2013], 382–399) has observed that, in the early Church, the novelty of

Christian forgiveness was such that it even required the development of a new vocabulary:

> Why is there no intellectual or literary "creep" — no evidence that pre-existing, Hellenistic ideas to do with forgiveness are in evidence in the New Testament? [Because] early Christians considered Christian forgiveness to be categorically different from the way people had previously understood and practiced forgiveness. … To borrow and adapt a metaphor from the Gospels, the New Testament writers resisted putting new wine in old wineskins. (395)

2. As we will see further ahead, when it comes to the how-to of forgiveness, this act of the will, as a response to the prompting of grace, and supported by grace, must also be bolstered by the emotions. Forgiveness is closely related to emotions of compassion and empathy which will often (or typically) be involved in triggering the will to forgive.

3. Anger is a normal first reaction to emotional harm. It can resolve itself into a desire for justice — for reasonable vengeance. As Thomas Aquinas observes: "To wish evil to someone under the aspect of justice may be according to the virtue of justice if it be in conformity with the order of reason; and anger fails only in this, that it does not obey the precept of reason in taking vengeance" (Thomas Aquinas, *Summa Theologiae*, I-II, q. 46, a.6c).

4. Not without reason do victims of sexual abuse (all the more, victims of abuse by clergy) easily refer to their ordeal as "soul murder." (See Thomas Berg, *Hurting in the Church* [Huntington, IN: OSV, 2017], chapter 2, "Soul Murder.")

5. Validation and acceptance are components of the psychological concept known as "affirmation." The psycho-theological reality of affirmation, as defined by Catholic psychiatrist Conrad Baars, refers to the "affective capacity to be moved by the good of the other, which normally precedes and enriches the effective activity of lovingly doing what is good for the other"

(Conrad W. Baars, *I Will Give Them a New Heart: Reflections on the Priesthood and the Renewal of the Church*, eds. Suzanne M. Baars and Bonnie N. Shayne [Staten Island, NY: St. Paul's/Alba House, 2008], 190). Baars continues, "Authentic affirmation is much more than speaking a word of encouragement or the giving of a compliment. *It focuses on the very being of the other, on his or her goodness as a unique human being.* It presupposes openness, confident expectation and uninterrupted attention to everything that happens in the other, to all the person is not able to express, and to all the anticipated good within the other, even though the other is still unsuspecting of that future good" (p. 14, italics in the original). Baars notes, "Everyone receives his or her physical existence from a mother and a father. Every person must also be born psychologically, however, and this only happens as a result of the affirming presence of [another]. For the one affirmed, it is their psychic or psychological birth; and for the affirming person, it is the opportunity to co-create with God" (68–69).

6. A recent review in the interdisciplinary journal *Pain* concluded that validation has a positive impact on one's emotional state, and invalidation has a negative impact on one's emotional state (Edmond & Keefe, 2015). Two examples are offered to see the impact of validation, and invalidation, on another. One study found that "participants exposed to invalidating responses experienced significantly higher levels of negative affect, heart rate, and skin conductance over time when compared to participants exposed to validating responses." See C. E. Shenk and A. E. Fruzzetti, "The Impact of Validating and Invalidating Responses on Emotional Reactivity," *Journal of Social and Clinical Psychology* 30, no. 2 (2011): 163–183.

Another study found that in individuals who experience physical pain, validation decreased their experience of the pain whereas invalidation increased their heart rate. See E. A. Kaufman, M. E. Puzia, A. Donald, A. Godfrey, and S. E. Crowell, "Physiological and behavioral effects of interpersonal validation: A multilevel approach to examining a core intervention strategy among self-injuring adolescents and their mothers," *Journal of Clinical Psychology* 76 (2020): 559–580.

Chapter 2: Maybe the Hardest Case of All

1. Vitz and Meade, approaching the issue as clinical therapists, argue that "self-forgiveness" is a misleading and inaccurate concept in the clinical setting, and argue instead for employing the notion of "self-acceptance." They suggest that self-forgiveness is unnecessary if the person could receive forgiveness from the Lord. Self-forgiveness, they argue, promotes narcissism. See P. C. Vitz and J. M. Meade, "Self-forgiveness in psychology and psychotherapy: A critique," *Journal of Religion and Health* 50 (2011): 248–263.

Fitzgibbons echoes these concerns, particularly applied to couples therapy: "Self-forgiveness fosters the major enemy of marital love — selfishness. It minimizes both the harm one has inflicted and the need one has to be forgiven by God and others." R. Fitzgibbons, *Habits for a Healthy Marriage: A Handbook for Catholic Couples* (San Francisco: Ignatius Press, 2019), 51. For additional pitfalls of self-forgiveness, see M. J. A. Wohl and K. J. McLaughlin, "Self-forgiveness: The good, the bad and the ugly," *Social and Personality Psychology Compass* 8, no. 8 (2014): 422–435. Nevertheless, most recent scientific research is attempting to address these concerns and is differentiating self-forgiveness that is repentant and humble, from self-forgiveness that is simply a justification of one's sinful behaviors. Most notably, Griffin and Worthington and their colleagues have articulated their Dual-Process Model of Self-Forgiveness that seeks to provide "a moral repair strategy in which perpetrators (a) reorient toward positive values by making a decision to accept responsibility for wrongdoing and align their behavior with positive values in the future as well as (b) restore esteem by replacing self-condemning emotions with self-affirming emotions." See B. J. Griffin, E. L. Worthington, D. E. Davis, J. N. Hook, and S. Maguen, "Development of the Self-Forgiveness Dual-Process Scale," *Journal of Counseling Psychology* 65 (2018): 716–717. For additional research on developing assessments and interventions to address both the interpersonal aspects as well as the intrapersonal aspects of genuine self-forgiveness, see S. E. McElroy-Heltzel, D. E. Davis, A. C. Ordaz, B. J. Griffin, and J. N. Hook, "Measuring forgiveness and self-forgiveness: Descriptions, psychometric support, and recommendations for research and practice," in E. L. Worthington and N. G. Wade, eds., *Handbook of Forgive-*

ness, 2nd ed. (New York: Routledge, 2020), 74–84; M. A. Cornish, B. J. Griffin, and G. W. Morris, "Promotion of self-forgiveness," Ibid., 288–298; A. Isacco and J. Wade, *Religion, Spirituality, and Masculinity: New Insights for Counselors* (New York: Routledge, 2019); and E. L. Worthington, *Forgiveness and Reconciliation: Theory and Application* (New York: Routledge, 2006).

2. We would hasten to point out, however, that not all persons who have suffered emotional trauma or perpetrated harm in the lives of others experience the need to forgive another or forgive themselves. Not out of a sense of self-degradation in the one case or narcissism in the other, but because under the influence of grace and the deep healing action of the Holy Spirit in their lives, forgiveness of any sort simply does not present itself as an issue. One might ask: Did Paul of Tarsus wrestle with self-forgiveness after having overseen the stoning of Stephen? We don't know what happened in the desert in those weeks following his conversion. Paul refers to himself as "the worst" of sinners (see 1 Timothy 1:15). Yet might it not be the case that the surpassing experience of personal redemption received at baptism was enough to mitigate and eliminate any lingering guilt or struggle, and to allow grace to unfold a new chapter in his life?

3. And that is because we are embodied spirits — neither purely angelic, nor purely animal. We're a hybrid: embodied consciousness. And this, in simple terms, is what allows us the freedom to transcend the limitations of our physical-material reality and, with our mind, turn back on, gaze at, and reflect upon the very self that is doing the turning back, gazing, and reflecting.

4. We base our considerations in large part on Curt Thompson's groundbreaking treatment of this topic in *The Soul of Shame: Retelling the Stories We Believe about Ourselves* (Downers Grove, IL: InterVarsity Press, 2015).

5. When accurate, guilt offers us a certain conscience check — it is that angel on our shoulder telling us we're doing something wrong. Yet we all know the experience when feeling guilt is inaccurate; when it does not reflect the environment. We feel guilty, but it is not warranted. We *feel guilty* when we enjoy something legitimate — and because it is legitimate, there is no need for guilt. Here we have to readjust our understanding and/or work through the feelings of unnecessary guilt.

6. Scientists who study trauma have differentiated two manifestations of traumatic events. A trauma that occurs once, like an automobile accident, has a beginning, a middle, and an end. A trauma occurring over a long period of time, like growing up with an alcoholic parent, extends back to one's earliest memory, and may not have ended (if the parent is still an active alcoholic). The one-time trauma causes the condition referred to as "posttraumatic stress disorder"; the long-term developmental trauma causes "complex posttraumatic stress disorder" or CPTSD.

With CPTSD, the personality structure has had to be modified to manage living in this constantly toxic environment; therefore, the individual's manner of interacting with the world is often maladaptive. This condition is imbued with shame because the individual feels as if he was somehow supposed to change his behavior to improve the environment. This is very common in children. Little children have the sense that they control the world: baby gets hungry and cries, and then gets fed. The world reacts to the little creature's pleas for help. This is the experience of the child, the emotional life of the child, and the self-talk of the child. The reader might have heard stories of little kids getting angry at dad, wishing dad would die — and then dad *does* die in a remarkable turn of events, and the devastated child believes that he killed his daddy.

This can come to shape the emotional reaction to sustained trauma in older children as well when things go wrong — such as dad drinking to the point of passing out, and the child attempting to take action to control the environment. No matter what the child does, the drinking behavior does not change. The child somehow feels responsible and therefore inadequate for being unable to stop the destructive behavior. The child feels at fault for the negative experiences in their family that are clearly, to an adult perspective, not the child's responsibility at all. Further, sometimes an adult will communicate the sense that the child is bad or blatantly tell a child, "You are bad."

7. Curt Thompson, *The Soul of Shame*, 140.

8. Ibid., 136–137.

Chapter 3: How Do You Know When You've Really Forgiven Someone?

1. God in his omnipotence does not literally "forget" our sins; but rather, it is in the superabundance of his mercy that, once we have repented, he no longer takes them into account. This means that, at our final judgment, the sins for which we will be held accountable are those sins for which we have not yet repented. It is on the basis of this wonderful truth, incidentally, that St. Thomas Aquinas taught the necessity of the seal of confession: "Now God hides the sins of those who submit to Him by Penance; wherefore this also should be signified in the sacrament of Penance, and consequently the sacrament demands that the confession should remain hidden (*ST*, Suppl., q.11)."

For Aquinas, the seal of confession has an important sign value, namely that it images for the Church the reality that God "hides the sins" of repentant sinners, obliterating memory of those sins. On this basis, a priest must never reveal the identity of a penitent and any sin he or she has confessed.

2. To understand how grace elevates and perfects human forgiveness, we might consider a similar dynamic Thomas Aquinas recognized as being at work in the virtues. Faith, hope, and love are called the "theological virtues" because their origin in us comes directly from God. They are *infused by God* into the soul at baptism. Human virtues on the other hand, or excellences of any sort — self-control, generosity, humility, honesty — are normally achieved through the repetition of acts, but they can be strengthened by grace as well. Once we perform the virtuous acts with relative ease, and desire the virtue as something good in itself, we can rightly be considered "virtuous" in that particular respect.

The theological virtues, however, do not come about in us in this way. They are gifts of grace. Yes, we freely cooperate with grace in order to grow in those virtues whose seed we received in baptism, but they are in the end God's free gift to us. Faith, hope, and love are received (infused in us) at baptism. And therefore, their presence, at least in the order of grace, distinguishes the baptized from the unbaptized. But the reality that all human beings are created in the image of God disposes us, we might say, to receive those gifts of grace. At the human level, belief, optimism, and goodness/kindness are, in a sense, corollaries of the infused virtues of faith, hope, and love.

St. Thomas Aquinas was convinced, however, that at least some human virtues are also infused by God. And he was thinking primarily of what the Tradition refers to as the "cardinal virtues": justice, prudence, fortitude, and temperance. It seems his understanding was that, given the presence of the infused theological virtues in us, we could not but recognize that certain human virtues *can also be subject to an infused counterpart.* Aquinas's understanding is that the very presence of the infused *theological* virtues in us must bring about, at the level of human virtues, a proportionate effect, namely, *infused* moral virtues (See *ST*, I-II, q. 63, a.3). In this way, grace can build on nature; and natural virtue can move toward perfection under the influence of grace. While forgiveness is not itself a virtue, the virtue of mercy assists the act of forgiveness, and in some sense forgiveness helps perfect the virtue of mercy. "Blessed are the merciful for mercy shall be theirs." So, in this light, it makes perfect sense to understand that human forgiveness can be elevated by grace, especially when directed by the infused virtue of prudence, and most of all perfected by the theological virtue of charity, of which mercy is an exalted expression — or as Aquinas would say, an inward effect of charity.

Chapter 4: Opening to Grace

1. See also 1 John 3:5 and 4:10.

2. Sermon 5 on the Lord's Prayer in *Ancient Christian Writers: The Works of the Fathers in Translation*, No. 18, St. Gregory of Nyssa — The Lord's Prayer & The Beatitudes (London: Longmans, Green and Co., 1954), 71 (slightly edited to update language).

3. Scott Hahn, "Forgive Us … As We Forgive," *Lay Witness* (March/April 2003).

4. It is the second of his "five keys" to deliverance: believing, forgiving, renouncing, taking authority, and receiving blessings. See Neal Lozano, *Unbound: A Practical Guide to Deliverance* (Grand Rapids, MI: Chosen Books, 2003).

5. Ibid., 78–79.

6. Benedict XVI, *Deus Caritas Est,* par. 18.

Chapter 5: The Key You've Been Looking For

1. See *ST*, I-II, q.46, a.1.

2. Thomas Aquinas, *De Malo*, a.11, "Does sin diminish the natural good?"

3. See Douglas Stone, Bruce Patton, and Sheila Heen, *Difficult Conversations: How to Discuss What Matters Most* (New York: Penguin, 1999), 113.

Chapter 6: So How Do We Do It?

1. Both scholars have websites that offer free materials, and Dr. Worthington's website offers free downloadable workbooks that walk the reader through the forgiveness process.

For more about Dr. Robert Enright's work, see
www.internationalforgiveness.com.

For more about Dr. Everett Worthington's work, see
www.evworthington-forgiveness.com.

2. A recent meta-analysis found that both the Enright Process Model of Interpersonal Forgiveness (R. D. Enright and R. P. Fitzgibbons, *Forgiveness Therapy: An Empirical Guide for Resolving Anger and Restoring Hope* [Washington, DC: American Psychological Association, 2015]) and the REACH Forgiveness Intervention (E. L. Worthington, Jr., "An update of the REACH Forgiveness model to promote forgiveness," in Everett L. Worthington, Jr. and Nathaniel G. Wade (Eds.), *Handbook of Forgiveness,* 2nd ed [New York: Routledge, 2020], 277–287) are scientifically efficacious in helping people forgive (N. G. Wade, W. T. Hoyt, J. E. M. Kidwell, and E. L. Worthington, "Efficacy of psycho-therapeutic interventions to promote forgiveness: A meta-analysis," *Journal of Consulting and Clinical Psychology* 74 (2014): 920–929). While there is significant overlap in the two approaches, the style of presentation is different. The Enright Process Model is an approach to forgiveness that we have utilized in this book. Enright's model offers four main segments: Uncovering Phase, Decision Phase,

Work Phase, and Deepening Phase. For the purposes of our book, we have slightly revised the names of the phases, and we refer to them as the four steps: Uncovering, Deciding, Proclaiming, and Deepening. The steps in this book correspond to Enright's phases. These phases are summarized most recently in the *Handbook of Forgiveness*, 2nd Edition. (S. Freedman and R. D. Enright, "A review of the empirical research using Enright's process model of interpersonal forgiveness," in E. L. Worthington and N. G. Wade, eds., *Handbook of Forgiveness*, 2nd edition [New York: Routledge, 2020], 266–276). Enright has also explained these steps extensively in various books (R. D. Enright, *The Forgiving life: A Pathway to Overcoming Resentment and Creating a Legacy of Love* [Washington, DC: American Psychological Association, 2012]; Enright and Fitzgibbons, 2015), as well as on his website, www.internationalforgiveness.com. In addition, we encourage the reader to visit Worthington's website to explore the many downloadable workbooks that are available for free, www.evworthington-forgiveness.com.

3. Conrad W. Baars, *I Will Give Them a New Heart*, 245.

4. "In time of desolation we should never make any change, but remain firm and constant in the resolution and decision which guided us the day before the desolation, or in the decision to which we adhered in the preceding consolation. For just as in consolation, the good spirit guides and counsels us, so in desolation the evil spirit guides and counsels. Following his counsels we can never find the way to a right decision." Spiritual Exercises, the 5th Rule for the Discernment of Spirits, n. 318, in Louis J. Puhl, SJ, The Spiritual Exercises of St. Ignatius, (The Newman Press, 1951 reprint edition by Loyola Press, 2021), 142–143.

5. Another common way that we can do this is through "expressive writing," a technique popularized by psychologist Dr. James Pennebaker, professor at the University of Texas at Austin. This line of research found that as people write about stressful, hurtful, and traumatic events in their past, and as they articulate their emotions and feel their feelings about the past, they begin to feel better in the present. Their anxiety and depression decrease. Their happiness and contentment increase. Beyond the psychological

impact, the research shows that people engaged in expressive writing show improvements in their immune system, decrease in physical illness, and improvement in school performance.

6. Baars, *I Will Give Them a New Heart*, 245–246.

Chapter 8: Going Even Deeper

1. Karen Edmisten, *You Can Share the Faith: Reaching Out One Person at a Time* (Huntington, IN: Our Sunday Visitor, 2016), 104.

2. While it is commonly seen as a time to mentally note the sins we've committed during the day, traditionally the examen was much more. First and foremost, it is an opportunity to see the presence of the Lord in our life and his movement in our heart and life during the day. The examen allows us to recognize his grace unfolding in our life and how we cooperated with that grace. In addition, the examen is an opportunity to take responsibility for when we did not cooperate with that grace. See the seminal article by George Aschenbrenner, SJ, "Consciousness Examen," in *The Hidden Self Grown Strong* (St. Joseph's Communications, 2018), 119–135; and also Timothy Gallagher, OMV, *The Examen Prayer: Ignatian Wisdom for Our Lives Today* (Crossroad, 2006).

3. Spiritual Exercises, n. 43. See Louis J. Puhl, SJ, trans., *The Spiritual Exercises of St. Ignatius* (The Newman Press, 1951, reprint edition by Loyola Press, 2021).

4. Pope Francis, *The Name of God is Mercy: A Conversation with Andrea Tornielli*, trans. Oonagh Stransky (New York: Random House, 2016), 41.

5. Pope Francis, General Audience, March 18, 2020.

6. Aschenbrenner, *The Hidden Self Grown Strong*, 84–85.

7. The Church has understood from the very beginning that the living out of the Christian moral life (the *lex vivendi*) flows out of the Church's life of prayer (the *lex orandi*). To be sure, this tight relationship is captured and expressed in the dismissal at the end of Mass. Although translated in different ways, the dismissal *"Ite, missa est"* literally means "Go, you are sent" — sent, as it were, through your choices and actions, to make good on the liturgical worship you have just participated in.

8. At the heart of the Old Law and perfected in the New Law is the project of ordering our lives toward worship. This is captured beautifully in specific teachings of Christ in which we grasp his own understanding of the profound and intrinsic unity of religious practice and moral practice which come together in Christian worship: "So if you are offering your gift at the altar, and there remember that your brother has something against you, leave your gift there before the altar and go; first be reconciled to your brother" (Mt 5:23–24, RSV-2CE).

Chapter 9: Saying "I Forgive You"

1. "An Act of Contrition," accessed September 17, 2021, https://www.ewtn.com/catholicism/devotions/act-of-contrition-338.

Afterword

1. See Stephen J. Pope, "The Promise of Restorative Justice," *America Magazine*, December 24, 2018. Our call as a community of disciples is to be, for victims of abuse, "a community of compassion and not just compensation."

2. Stephen J. Pope and Janine P. Geske, "Anger, Forgiveness, and Restorative Justice in Light of Clerical Sexual Abuse and Its Cover-up," *Theological Studies* 80, no. 3 (2019): 629.

3. Australian criminologist John Braithwaite critiques and further specifies that definition:

> Its main limitation is that it does not tell us who or what is to be restored. It does not define core values of restorative justice, which are about healing rather than hurting, moral learning, community participation and community caring, respectful dialogue, forgiveness, responsibility, apology, and making amends (see Nicholl 1998). I take those who have a "stake in a particular offense" to mean primarily the victim(s), the offender(s), and affected communities (which includes the families of victims and offenders). So restorative justice is about restoring victims, restoring offenders,

and restoring communities (Bazemore and Umbreit 1994; Brown and Polk 1996). One answer to the "What is to be restored?" question is whatever dimensions of restoration matter to the victims, offenders, and communities affected by the crime. Stakeholder deliberation determines what restoration means in a specific context. (John Braithwaite, *Restorative Justice & Responsive Regulation* [Oxford University Press, 2002], 11).

4. Aquinas holds, in fact, that anger (as opposed to hatred) is not only natural, but ultimately rational. Ever the observer of human nature, Aquinas himself understood — rather personally — that anger can be rightly ordered, that there is a reasonable manifestation of anger. This was doubtlessly bolstered, as Robert Miner has observed, by Aquinas's own brutal experience of having been imprisoned by his own family members who then sprang a prostitute on him in an attempt to keep him from following his vocation as a Dominican. Aquinas knew what it was to feel deep anger toward loved ones — an anger that was entirely reasonable. Not surprisingly, as Miner further observes, exploring the passion of anger in his *Summa* (I-II q. 46 especially in articles 4–6), Aquinas mounts a veritable *apologia pro ira*, a defense of anger against its critics. He holds that the object of anger is vindication (not unrelated to our contemporary notion of validation), that seeking vindication presupposes the use of reason, that vindication is a good worthy of reasonable pursuit, that when attained in a manner proportionate to the offense, it instantiates justice — which is also for the good of the perpetrator. But again, Aquinas is speaking here of anger — rightly ordered anger — and not hatred, which, especially in the context of the sexual abuse crisis, can often be confused with just anger. See Robert Miner, *Thomas Aquinas on the Passions* (Cambridge: Cambridge University Press, 2009), 268–286.

5. Geske and Pope very correctly note in fact that a relatively stable feeling of resentment toward the perpetrator can be compatible with forgiveness and with willing the good for the offender: "In some cases, proper self-regard, or willing the good for the self, may make it necessary for one to will the good to the offender while also acknowledging the legitimacy of one's own

resentment" (Geske and Pope, "Anger, Forgiveness, and Restorative Justice," 624–625).

6. Emily Ransom, "The Courage to Forgive After #MeToo," *Church Life Journal*, June 15, 2020, accessed September 17, 2021, https://churchlifejournal.nd.edu/articles/the-courage-to-forgive-after-metoo/.

7. While many in the Church recognize that a "vulnerable adult" can also be vulnerable due to the fact that there's a differential in power between the adult victim and their abuser, Canon Law continues to define "vulnerable adult" narrowly. It is common sense, however, to grasp, for example, that a woman who has gone through a difficult divorce, or a young adult dealing with anxiety and suicidal thoughts, or even in Emily's case, a well-educated and enthusiastic adult, an academic, and a recent convert to Catholicism — all are vulnerable to someone taking advantage of them who is in a position of trust and guidance, and in the case of clerics, who are set in a power differential due to the authority entrusted to them by the Church. Any adult can be vulnerable to sexual abuse where there is a differential of power between themselves and their abuser.

8. This is precisely the point that Margaret Farley has underlined as well:

> A descriptive analysis of the experience of forgiveness yields something like the following. To forgive is above all not to be passive in the face of injury, betrayal, persecution, abuse. Forgiveness may, in fact, be one of the most active responses possible in the face of whatever sort of breach occurs in human relationships. It is linguistically a "performative" — an utterance or gesture that signifies an action which accomplishes or at least aims to accomplish something ("Forgiveness in the Service of Love," in Fredrick V. Simmons, ed., *Love and Christian Ethics: Tradition, Theory and Society* [Washington: Georgetown University Press, 2016], 164.).

9. See Daniel Philpott, "Why the Catholic Church needs a Eucharistic response to the sex abuse scandals," *America*, February 20, 2019.

About the Authors

Fr. Thomas Berg is professor of moral theology and director of seminarian admissions at St. Joseph's Seminary in Yonkers, NY. In addition to his scholarly work in bioethics and moral theology, he has been a frequent public commentator on issues relating to the Catholic Church. In the past several years, he has frequently addressed issues relating to  the clergy sexual abuse crisis, the renewal of Catholic seminary formation, and the accompaniment of survivors of abuse. He is the author of *Hurting in the Church: A Way Forward for Wounded Catholics* (OSV, 2017).

 **Dr. Timothy Lock** is a Catholic father, husband, Franciscan Tertiary, clinical psychologist, and professional speaker. He is the founder and director of the Goretti Center for Healing and Forgiveness where he has been providing psychotherapy for over twenty years. Since 2019, Dr. Lock has been the full-time Director of Psychological Services at St. Joseph's Seminary (Dunwoodie) of the Archdiocese of New York. In addition to providing counseling, he has been involved with research, teaching, and seminary formation. Dr. Lock lives with his wife of twenty-eight years and their eight children in northwestern Connecticut.